DOUBLE!

New Meanings for an Old Bid

by
Mike Lawrence

ISBN: 0-9762999-0-9

Published by   MikeWorks
Brentwood, TN
(615) 221-9952

Table of Contents

INTRODUCTION

Good bridge players are a dime a dozen, and even a fine player can be had for a few hundred dollars a day -- if you're willing to shell out to hire one as a tournament partner. But world champions who can speak with weight of authority on every area of the game and write with economy and style are priceless commodities. Among those elite few, nobody surpasses my friend Mike Lawrence, and that makes the book you are holding the biggest bargain since the Alaska Purchase: You are about to share Mike's encyclopedic knowledge of bidding theory and benefit from his ease in articulating ideas. In "Doubles," Mike has treated every aspect of what has become the most flexible call in the auction.

Mike's first book, I recall, came about almost by accident. The late Ira Corn, captain of the Dallas Aces, prevailed on Mike to write something on card-placing. The result was "How to Read Your Opponents' Cards," which has remained a classic for 30 years. Mike has since produced more than a dozen other books, and it is a testament to his skills that every one has been of high quality and has added something valuable to the literature.

Double! is yet another superb Lawrence piece of work, and I feel honored that Mike asked me to write its introduction. Enjoy it and learn from it.

Frank Stewart
Fayette, Alabama

PREFACE

About eight years ago, I wrote *Takeout Doubles*. In the years since I have heard normal feedback about it, but beginning three years ago I started hearing, "Where is the sequel?" It seems that right there on the front cover of *Takeout Doubles* I stated that it was the first in a series of books on doubles. Well, it seemed like a good idea then and it is still a good idea. Here is the sequel.

This book covers all kinds of doubles, ranging from penalty doubles to Maximal Doubles to Support Doubles to some old favorites like Negative Doubles and Responsive Doubles, along with some doubles that are fresh off of the assembly line. In addition, there is a section on redoubles, one of the more underused bids in bridge. This is a brief section but should not be ignored.

ALERT!

Many of the conventions in this book are alertable. Be sure to alert if you use any of the doubles or other special bids in this book unless you are certain that it falls under the ACBL guidelines for a double that is not an alert, such as the Negative Double. In general, it is better to over-alert and learn which doubles are not alertable than the other way around.

CONVENTIONAL DOUBLES WHEN YOU OPEN THE BIDDING

The list of conventional doubles available to the side that opened the bidding used to number zero. Now there is a long list, from the everyday Negative Double to the relatively obscure Thrump Double. These doubles are divided into three categories: doubles after you have opened with one of a suit, after you have opened one or two notrump, and after you have opened with a strong two clubs.

WHEN YOUR SIDE OPENS ONE OF A SUIT

Negative Double

This is one convention that has been written about extensively. I do not intend to discuss this in depth when I can go to my library and find entire books devoted to it. I would mention the authors and names of these books but for the fact that if I overlooked one, I would hear about it. Let me say that you can find excellent references on this convention in bridge literature and leave it at that.

I will, however, look at a few questions that I have been asked in my classes. Most questions are doorways to other considerations and when necessary, I will address them too.

W	N	E	S
1♣	1◇	?	

How many hearts does East need to bid one heart? How about spades?

East needs four hearts to bid one heart and similarly, four spades to bid one spade. East cannot double one diamond without four cards in each major. This means that East may have to bid a pretty poor four card suit on some hands.

♠63 ♡J863 ◇9653 ♣AQ4

East must bid one heart. Since he does not have four spades, a Negative Double is out of the question.

RULE—*Four cards in both majors are needed to double a one diamond overcall.*

If there are two unbid majors, does a Negative Double always promise four cards in each major?

No. It is fine to make a Negative Double with just one of the two unbid majors on some auctions. I will show you examples shortly. Keep in mind that after a one diamond overcall, you do need both majors to double.

♠7653 ♡AJ76 ◇QJ4 ♣108

Double. You have both majors. Since the bidding is at the one level, you actually have a little bit more than you need. A fair six high card points is sufficient to bid at the one level.

What if you are five-four in the majors after that one diamond overcall? Should you double with these hands too?

It is OK to double with five-four in the majors too. This is one of the least discussed issues regarding Negative Doubles after a one diamond overcall. Take the following hands. Do you think they are better handled by doubling or bidding your long suit?

W	N	E	S
1♣	1♢	?	

♠AJ73 ♡J8543 ♢543 ♣3

It is hard to prove what is best, but experience suggests that doubling is better than bidding one heart. If you bid one heart and the next player bids two diamonds, you may lose a spade fit.

♠KJ973 ♡Q543 ♢53 ♣Q3

Double with this too. The same arguments apply. If you bid one spade and South can raise diamonds, you may lose a heart fit.

Admittedly, doubling is not perfect. If you double and your partner bids two clubs, rebidding his minor, you will have a difficult choice between passing and bidding two spades. This is not a perfect world.

♠KJ73 ♡AQ762 ♢32 ♣82

Double. This hand is almost strong enough that bidding one heart is best.

How strong a hand can you have with five-four in the majors before it is right to bid your long suit instead of doubling?

Believe it or not, I do not know if there is an industry standard for this question. I have a bridge library that has eight or nine shelves of books and not one offers an answer to this one. None of my friends had an answer they seemed to like so the following suggestion is the sum of a few vague opinions.

If you have a game forcing hand or about eleven good high card points with five-four in the majors, you should bid your long major. If you have less than this, start with double.

♠AQ63 ♡KQ1083 ♢76 ♣83

Bid one heart. No matter how the bidding goes you should be able to get spades into the bidding, thus ensuring you find the right suit at the right level. This hand is not really worth a game forcing bid, but it is close enough that bidding one heart is best. Add a point or two and it is clear to bid one heart instead of doubling.

Can you have five-five in the majors to double a one diamond overcall?

No. With five-five, always bid one spade. Usually you will have a second chance. I agree that this guideline will fail you once in awhile, but it will survive more often than not.

♠J10764 ♡KJ873 ◇73 ♣3

Bid one spade. You hope for a second chance. If you double and your partner does not have a four card major, you may not find your best five-three fit.

W	N	E	S
1♣	1♡	?	

This auction has a few special problems of its own.

Does a one spade bid promise four or five spades?

The most popular treatment bids one spade with five or more spades and makes a Negative Double with only four. This helps your partner in competitive auctions.

Be aware that there is another school that says double should be takeout for the unbid minor. This school bids one spade with four or more spades. I do not use this approach, but I can see the reasoning for it. It has merit.

Bidding Trick

W	N	E	S
1♣	1♡	Dbl	2♡
Pass	Pass	2♠	

This is an odd-looking auction. If it came up at the table, would you know what East was doing?

A nice agreement to have for this bid is that East is showing four spades along with support for opener's minor suit and limit raise values. On the sequence here, East is showing something like this hand.

♠Q984 ♡43 ◇KJ4 ♣AJ63

Using two spades in this way does three good things. It lets you show your values (it is barely possible that you have a game and if so, you have a chance to reach it). It lets you stop in the right partscore (your partner can choose between clubs and spades). And, on hands where you bid three clubs, you show that you are just competing.

♠Q983 ♡432 ◇87 ♣AQ74

This hand would bid three clubs over their two hearts. Your partner will understand that you have a modest hand only, because with a good ten or eleven point club hand, you would have bid two spades.

Remember this trick only exists when they overcall one heart. It does not exist when they overcall one diamond or one spade.

W	N	E	S
1◇	2♣	?	

If East doubles two clubs, does he promise both majors?

No. East can double with just one major but he'd better be careful.

RULE—*If you double on an auction like this one with just one of the unbid majors, you need a good enough hand that you can escape should your partner bid the major suit you do not have.*

Here are some examples using the auction above.

♠Q874 ♡A1042 ◇Q7 ♣763

This is a minimum Negative Double. You could double a one diamond overcall without the queen of diamonds but you should not come in at the two level with less than this.

♠73 ♡AQ74 ◇874 ♣J653

Pass. You expect your partner to bid spades and you can't stand for that to happen. It is bad enough if he bids two spades, but if he should bid three spades or four spades, it would be even worse.

♠J1073 ♡Q8 ◇A742 ♣KJ3

This is a possible hand for double. If your partner bids hearts, you will bid notrump. If he bids spades, the suit you like, you can raise.

♠J3 ♡AJ83 ◇KJ104 ♣763

This is another hand with only one major that is good enough to double with. If your partner bids spades, you will run to diamonds. You would prefer he only bid two spades so that you can bid three diamonds, but no matter what he does, you have a home of sorts in diamonds.

RULE—*If you make a Negative Double without the right shape, you need eleven or so points, either in notrump values or in support of your partner's minor suit.*

♠KJ1084 ♡A7 ◇J53 ♣1094

You might double with this hand too. Your wish would be to bid two spades if partner bids two diamonds or two hearts. If your partner bids three hearts, you still have to bid three spades but you would be less happy to do so.

♠A6 ♡KJ1063 ◇J63 ♣1063

Pass. This hand is tempting but does not offer a safe bid. Although I play that a two heart bid here is not game forcing,

14

even if playing Two Over One methods, this hand is not strong enough by my standards. On the previous hand with five spades, you could double and then bid spades. With this equivalent hand, doubling first is bad because you will very often have to contend with a two spade bid from partner.

How high should you play Negative Doubles?

I have seen them played up to two spades and up to seven spades. This last range is something of a joke, of course. In practice, using Negative Doubles up to four hearts is about as high as one would want to go. If you are just taking up Negative Doubles, I suggest you include them up to two spades. Later you should increase the level to four diamonds or even four hearts, but not higher.

I think that the most important thing is to agree with your partner how high these are played. Incidentally, if you decide to use Responsive Doubles too, you should play them up to the same level as Negative Doubles. Makes for easy memory.

Don't Be Greedy.

Here is a trap you do not want to fall into.

East-West Vulnerable

W	N	E	S
		1♡	3♣
?			

♠QJ2 ♡J3 ◇AQJ6 ♣KJ108

The situation is easy to define. You have a great hand, and they have bid to the three level. If you pass, and partner reopens with a double, you will reap a fortune. But what if your partner decides to pass it out? Here is the layout that you fear.

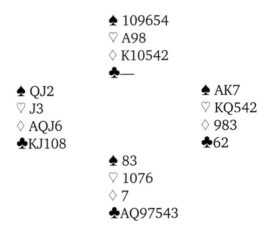

♠ 109654
♡ A98
◇ K10542
♣—

♠ QJ2   ♠ AK7
♡ J3   ♡ KQ542
◇ AQJ6   ◇ 983
♣KJ108   ♣62

♠ 83
♡ 1076
◇ 7
♣AQ97543

If you pass and your partner doubles, you can pass and set it four tricks for eight hundred points. However if your partner also decides to pass, you only get two hundred points. If you bid three notrump, you will make four for six hundred and thirty points. So take the pressure off of partner and bid three notrump.

If I had the East hand, I would not reopen, and I would expect many to agree with that choice. After all, if West has a different hand, bidding would be a disaster. Here is a look at another potential layout.

♠ QJ2   ♠ AK7
♡ 108   ♡ KQ542
◇ Q1052   ◇ 983
♣J973   ♣62

Should East reopen with his hand and find West with the hand above, there is nowhere to go.

The Negative Doubler's Later Bids

W	N	E	S
1♡	1♠	Dbl	2♠
Pass	Pass	?	

Opener Does Not Make a Rebid

When you make a Negative Double and your partner does not bid over South's raise, you know opener is minimum. What does it show if you double again? Since you are forcing the auction to continue, often at the three level, you need a ten point hand or better. These hands show some examples of second round bids.

♠Q1094 ♡3 ◇QJ86 ♣KJ84

You should pass. A double on the second round is not for penalty, it just says you are maximum for your earlier double. If you double again, your partner will strive to take it out.

♠874 ♡43 ◇AJ98 ♣KQJ10

Double. Perfect. Your first double ostensibly said you had seven or more points and both minors. Your second double repeats the earlier message and says you have a couple of points more than you showed with the first double. This hand is a point stronger than it needs to be.

W	N	E	S
1♣	1◇	Dbl	2◇
Pass	Pass	?	

♠A1074 ♡KJ874 ◇84 ♣J10

Bid two hearts. If you double and then bid a major suit on the exact sequence shown here, you promise a hand in the nine to eleven range with four cards in the other major and five in the bid major. This is not forcing. If you had enough to force, you would bid one heart on the first round and then follow up accordingly on this round.

Remember this one special sequence, which I discussed previously. It is different from the one above in that the overcall was one heart, not one diamond.

W	N	E	S
1♣	1♡	Dbl	2♡
Pass	Pass	2♠	

East denies five spades. Remember that East is showing four spades and a limit raise for clubs. This way he gets to clubs or spades according to what West has and also keeps the bidding low, important when West has a minimum hand.

If you are playing Negative Doubles, does opener have to reopen if an overcall is passed back to him?

W	N	E	S
1◇	1♡	Pass	Pass
?			

This sequence has penalty written all over it. Many good results come from opener doubling and responder sitting for it. This is the kind of thing that can occur.

Both Sides Vulnerable

```
                    ♠ AK3
                    ♡ KJ753
                    ◇ J73
                    ♣94
  ♠ Q984                        ♠ J62
  ♡ 8                           ♡ AQ1062
  ◇ AK1084                      ◇ Q9
  ♣A86                          ♣QJ7
                    ♠ 1075
                    ♡ 94
                    ◇ 652
                    ♣K10532
```

West opens one diamond and North comes in with one heart. If using Negative Doubles, East will pass and West will reopen

with a double. East passes, and North gets to play an ugly
contract. On good defense North will get a couple of spades
and a heart. Maybe two hearts. At best he goes down eight
hundred and at worst, he goes down eleven hundred.

On this hand West has a clear reopening double. His shape
suggests that East has some hearts and the opponents' quiet
bidding suggests that East also has some points. A reopening
double by West is automatic on hands like this one.

Now the question I asked earlier. When the bidding starts as
above, does West have to reopen or can he pass it out? I know
some players who have a rule about this. Their rule is that
opener MUST bid in this situation. This is madness, of course.
Rules are nice but judgment has to come into play too. Give
West this hand.

♠Q4 ♡Q1062 ◇AQ54 ♣KJ6

After opening one diamond, North overcalls one heart and East
passes. Must West bid if South passes? The answer is no. Here
is the proof. Can East have a heart stack looking for a penalty?
He can not. You have four good hearts, and North has a good
suit, too. Since East does not have hearts he would have bid if
he had something to bid. Here is a likely layout.

♠ AJ3
♡ AK753
◇ 9
♣A432

♠ Q4		♠ K102
♡ Q1062		♡ 984
◇ AQ54		◇ J762
♣KJ6		♣1085

♠ 98765
♡ J
◇ K1083
♣Q97

Is this a possible layout? I think so. North has a sound one heart bid, East has nothing to say, and South has a hand that most would pass with.

What happens if West bids? Firstly, one has to ask just what West should bid. Double is silly since West has no spade suit. One notrump is worse since the bid promises about eighteen points. East has promised nothing so West's bidding one notrump with a boring minimum is a big overbid.

Look what happens if West doubles. East will bid two diamonds and North will make a takeout double when that comes back to him. South will bid spades and North-South will have found their best trump suit.

East and West have a small chance of setting one heart. They have no chance of setting two spades. Not a terrible disaster, but not good bridge. By the way. I could have made the example even more scary. I could have given you a layout where North-South bid and make four spades after having stopped in one heart.

The question was whether opener had to reopen after an overcall was passed around to him. The answer is that opener has to use his judgment and not a silly rule that says reopening is mandatory.

OPENER'S RETURN NEGATIVE DOUBLE

W	N	E	S
1♣	1♡	Dbl	2♡
Dbl			

What does opener's double mean? Is it penalty? Is it takeout? Is it something else?

A convention that is not well known is the Return Negative Double. It occurs when your partner makes a Negative Double and your RHO raises. On the auction above, opener's double of two hearts is takeout. Opener promises something like the following hand.

♠QJ8 ♡2 ◇AJ87 ♣AQJ87

Assuming you would open one club with this hand, you know that you have enough to bid on over two hearts, but the bid you choose is important. You know East has exactly four spades so bidding those is not that exciting. Spades could be right, however, so you do not want to lose them entirely. You could belong in diamonds and you could belong in clubs. The trouble is that if you bid three clubs or three diamonds, you risk being in the wrong suit.

The answer is to double. You need the agreement that this is not a penalty double but a takeout double and if you have this agreement, it will get you through this hand comfortably.

How does your partner bid in response to your double?

For starters, he knows you want him to bid and he knows you have about fifteen useful points or more. He also knows you do not have four spades because you would have bid them at some level if you did. Here are some examples of hands he can have. Remember that opener's hand is the one shown above. You can refer back to it to see how your choice will work out.

♠K1074 ♡K73 ◇Q64 ♣953

Bid two spades. With no liking for clubs or diamonds, East chooses two spades, which rates to be a quiet partscore. East knows he is playing in a four-three fit. NOTE that he does not bid notrump. Two notrump would show around ten points.

♠10763 ♡J543 ◇K10 ♣K93

Bid three clubs. You might bid two spades if you wish to play in what will be a nervous four-three fit. NOTE that your partner will not play you for five spades.

♠A742 ♡873 ◇K1093 ♣64

Bid three diamonds. One thing is clear here. Your partner has four diamonds and three spades. He rates to have five clubs too. I can imagine he has a hand with 3-2-4-4 shape that wants to compete but it more likely he has five clubs.

♠10753 ♡K98 ◇KQ3 ♣K104

Two notrump is OK with this. You might even bid three notrump since opener is marked with a good hand.

♠AK104 ♡J74 ◇652 ♣K64

This one may be a bit fanciful but four spades is the winning contract. Perhaps the right bid with this hand is three spades, catering to a known four-three fit, but doing so intelligently. Since you can actually make five spades with most normal lines of play, and might make six on occasion, getting to spades is a very big deal. Here is what the two hands look like again.

♠ QJ8	♠ AK104
♡ 2	♡ J74
◇ AJ87	◇ 652
♣AQJ87	♣K64

Ten easy tricks in spades, perhaps eleven or even twelve tricks in spades. Only ten tricks in clubs.

♠A652 ♡QJ107 ◇Q52 ♣63

How about passing for penalty? You know partner has extra values, you know your side does not have a good spade fit, and you know that you do not have a good fit in either minor either. You should set them two or more tricks, and if it turns out that the cards are so well-placed that you can make three notrump, it will turn out that the cards are also well placed for defense. You might, on a good day, set two hearts three or four tricks.

Here is another example of this treatment.

	♠ AJ4		♠ Q872	
	♡ KJ6		♡ A852	
	◇ 73		◇ 86	
	♣KQ1076		♣J95	

W	N	E	S
1♣	1◇	Dbl	2◇
Dbl	Pass	3♣	Pass
Pass	Pass		

East makes a Negative Double of North's one diamond bid and South raises to two diamonds. What should West do? Many players would pass but West does have a nice hand that ought to be safe in some partscore. If West can double for takeout, he stays in contention to find a five-three major suit fit, a club fit, or at worst, a four-three major suit fit.

West can double without misleading partner about his major suits, because he would always bid a major if he had a four card suit. The double must be showing two three card majors and long clubs. Personally, I cannot imagine a hand that would double with 3-3-3-4 shape so West's five card club suit is more or less a given. At the table, a likely result is that their side will compete to three diamonds where you have a chance to get a plus score on defense.

Should you use this Return Negative Double treatment? I would say so. Considering that using double as penalty is almost never going to happen (I can't remember using it that way for years) and considering that it will help you with many nice hands that do not have clear direction, I give this treatment a strong vote.

One Last Look at Opener's Return Negative Double

Before leaving this topic, I would like to address one additional auction.

W	N	E	S
1♣	1♠	Dbl	2♠
Dbl			

What should West's double show?

You can play that double is takeout along the lines of the hands I showed above. Opener should have something like this hand.

♠8 ♡AJ3 ◇QJ84 ♣AKJ83

Or you can play that double is takeout but with this extra proviso. If you double and bid hearts, you show a competitive hand, not a good hand.

♠74 ♡AJ84 ◇K3 ♣A10953

This hand wants to compete in hearts but does not want to excite partner. If using the agreement shown here, you can double and hope that the auction does not get out of hand. Ideally, your partner will bid something at the three level and you will be able to bid three hearts.

If you choose to bid three hearts directly over two spades you show a good hand.

♠3 ♡AQ84 ◇Q94 ♣AK1094

This hand would raise a one heart response to three hearts. These values are about right to bid three hearts directly in the arrangement shown above.

THE FLAW—If you use double and then three hearts to show a weakish hand, you are at the mercy of the opponents should they bid something that stops you from showing your hand. It can happen.

THRUMP DOUBLE

I must admit that I had never heard of a Thrump Double until I was spending time with a friend in Canada, and our conversation turned to players he knew. One of them was Marty Bergen, whose convention Bergen Raises can be found on many convention cards. One thing led to another and the next thing I knew, my friend was asking me what I thought of Bergen's Thrump Double.

It is embarrassing when you do not know what someone is talking about. It seems that the Thrump Double is something that was invented by Eric Rodwell and touted strongly by Marty Bergen. It works this way. Your partner opens with one of any suit and your RHO bids three of any other suit. The Thrump Double does not ask partner to bid a suit, it asks partner if he can bid three notrump. Here is the ideal hand.

W	N	E	S
	1♢	3♡	?

♠J5 ♡73 ◇K4 ♣AKQ8763

What should you bid? If you are using Negative Doubles, a double risks getting your partner excited about spades. And, if you bid four clubs, you get your side beyond three notrump, the spot you most want to know about.

The Thrump Double works wonders on this hand. With a heart stopper, North bids three notrump and you are happy. If he does not have a stopper, he bids whatever looks appropriate. (No one ever says what to do when their favorite convention does not function as wished.)

♠KQ63 ♡3 ◇KQ4 ♣KJ853

You are supposed to double with this hand too. If North bids three notrump you know he has hearts stopped, but you have no idea if three notrump is a good contract. Say he has this hand, for instance.

♠J1084 ♡A9 ◇AJ108 ♣Q94

You are more or less cold for four spades, and in three notrump, you rate to go down four. In this case, the Thrump Double was not so hot.

I spoke briefly with Marty about this and he says that in his experience, the Thrump Double is a winner. I am not yet convinced, but then I have not had a chance to test it. Definitely worth thinking about, however.

SUPPORT DOUBLE

In almost any bidding sequence, knowing how many trumps your partner has will be useful. In the following auction, West's raise does not promise four trumps. Anyone who has read my opinions about bidding knows that I strongly advocate raising with just three card support when a better bid is not available. Many good things come of this style, but I do admit that hands like this one suffer a little as a result.

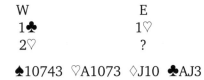

W	E
1♣	1♡
2♡	?

♠10743 ♡A1073 ◇J10 ♣AJ3

If opener has a maximum with four card support, you may have a game if the hands fit well. If opener has three trumps, a partscore is probably right, regardless of whether partner has a minimum or a maximum. The most important ingredient in your decision-making is how many trumps partner has for his raise. *Is there a way to solve this?*

Curiously, there is no good way to handle this in an uncontested auction, but there is a way to solve some of the bidding problems when the opponents compete.

W	N	E	S
		1♦	Pass
1♥	1♠	2♥	2♠
?			

♠873 ♥KJ84 ♦AQ2 ♣J72

What do you think West should bid over South's two spades? Admit it. You want to bid, but the correct choice is uncertain. I will tell you one of two things. You choose which one you want me to tell you.

1.   I will tell you how many hearts East has.
2.   I will tell you how many points East has.

Which do you want to know? Don't you agree that the number of trumps he has is twice as useful to you as the number of points? How can you get this information at the table? The answer is to use Support Doubles and Redoubles.

How Support Doubles and Redoubles Work

The Support Double works this way. You open and your partner bids a suit at the one level. Let us assume for the moment that partner has bid a major suit. Your RHO either overcalls or makes a takeout double. For example:

W	N	E	S
1♣	P	1♥	2♦
?			

W	N	E	S
1♣	P	1♥	Dbl
?			

On the first auction, using the Support Double, you can raise your partner in two ways. You can raise or you can double. The second auction is similar; you can raise or redouble. In either auction, with four card support, you raise to two, three, or four hearts according to the value of your hand. You might also make a splinter bid with the right values.

If you have three card support, you can show this fact by doubling two diamonds in the first auction or redoubling in the second. I expect you to forget this once. The ensuing turmoil will cure you of forgetting twice. If this does happen to you, don't give up. The Support Double is a good convention and is worth the trouble to remember.

W	N	E	S
1♣	Pass	1♡	2◇
2♡			

When you raise partner directly over the opponent's intervening bid or double, he will know how many points you have since you can raise to the two, three, or four level.

W	N	E	S
1♣	Pass	1♡	2◇
Dbl			

However, when you double or redouble to show three card support, you do not describe the value of your hand. You show partner that you have three card support but you do not limit your hand. You may have a minimum hand or any one of various kinds of bigger hands. If you have a big hand, you usually start with a double showing your three card support and then bid again to further define your hand.

You may double two diamonds with all of these hands. Note that in some cases you intend to bid again.

♠KJ74 ♡Q106 ◇87 ♣AQ105

Double. You do not promise a big hand with this double. All you promise is three card support. You happen to have four spades too. Just a coincidence. It would be nice if you could show those too, but it cannot be done. At the very least, you do get to tell partner about your support. Let's say that North raises to three diamonds and your partner goes on to three hearts. Isn't it nice to know that your partner knows you have three trump?

♠Q73 ♡975 ◇Q7 ♣AKJ105

If you are wondering whether the Support Double is mandatory, I give you this hand. I believe you can use your judgment about this. With three little hearts and the doubtful queen of diamonds, I can see passing. If the queen of diamonds were the queen of hearts, I would double. Doubling is OK on bare minimum hands as long as all the points are working.

♠AQ3 ♡K82 ◇A92 ♣KQJ3

With Support Doubles, you can have the best of two worlds. You want to bid two notrump to show the nineteen points, but you also want to show some heart support. You can double here to show the support and then, on the next round, you will bid two notrump to show a big hand. This gives your partner a nice inference when you bid two notrump directly over two diamonds. He will know you do not have heart support and will judge accordingly.

♠73 ♡AKJ ◇72 ♣AKQ863

This is another hand that qualifies for a special trick. Double, showing the three card support, and then bid three clubs to show a big hand with clubs. Compare this hand with the next.

♠86 ♡KQ8 ◇J10 ♣AQ7642

You can make a Support Double over two diamonds. However, if the bidding continues, you must not volunteer three clubs. If you make a Support Double and bid again, you show a good hand.

When you redouble to show three card support, things are the same as on auctions where you use double to show three card support. You redouble on any range of hand that has three card support and later show if your hand has extra values.

♠A73 ♡J83 ◇72 ♣AQJ63

You would redouble and then pass your partner's next bid unless he forced you to bid again.

♠AJ4 ♡J84 ◇AQJ ♣KQ108

Redouble and follow, most likely, with two notrump.

♠83 ♡AQJ ◇73 ♣AKQ874

Redouble and later rebid clubs if the auction allows it. These principles are the same as those that exist after you use a double to show three card support.

Some Auctions That Need Discussion

If you agree to play Support Doubles, you must decide how high to play them and you must also discuss whether they apply when the opponents bid notrump or make a cue bid. I suggest you play Support Doubles on every conceivable auction up to the level of two of responder's suit. It makes for easy remembering. Some examples:

W	N	E	S
1♣	Pass	1♡	1♠
Dbl			

This is the standard Support Double auction.

W	N	E	S
1♣	1◇	1♡	1♠
Dbl			

Even though both opponents have bid, the Support Double remains in place.

W	N	E	S
1♣	1◇	1♡	1NT
Dbl			

When South bids notrump, there is some logic in playing double is for penalty. I suggest you continue to play it as support, though. If your partner feels strongly about this, it is one of the few areas where I can see keeping the penalty orientation. For me, the Support Double has enough validity that I am happy to keep it.

W	N	E	S
1♣	1♡	1♠	2♡
Dbl			

When the opponents have bid and raised, Support Doubles are as important as ever. The auction is likely to speed up, costing you bidding room. Even if you play that one spade shows five of them, East will appreciate knowing how many spades you have.

W	N	E	S
1♣	1♡	1♠	2♣
Dbl			

South's two clubs is announced as a cue bid in support of hearts. It is tempting to double this whenever you have real clubs, but you know that they are going to at least two hearts and maybe higher. It is sensible to play that doubling two clubs shows support for spades. As stated earlier, I think it is OK to play that all doubles are support since it makes for easy memory considerations.

W	N	E	S
1♣	Pass	1♠	2♠
Dbl			

You will rarely hear South cue-bidding your partner's suit. When you hear this auction, you need to know what it means. Some South players play that this cue bid is natural (I recommend this treatment). Others play that two spades is some kind of two-suited cue bid.

When the cue bid is artificial, whether two-suited or something else, Support Doubles make sense. However, when the cue bid is natural, a very sensible treatment, it will show a pretty good six card suit. This is a very difficult moment for your side. Opener is almost never going to have enough cards in the suit to want to double for penalty. I suggest that you play that double is Negative, showing a good hand but denying the cue-bid suit.

♠2 ♡AQ84 ◇KQ7 ♣AJ1076

Referring to the previous auction, your double says you wish to compete but don't know exactly how to do it. Your partner can pass in a pinch but should bid a new suit or raise opener without good cards in his suit. This takeout treatment has a lot to offer. A word to the wise here. The chances that you will have a chance to use this treatment are slim. I used to play double was for penalty but it never came up.

W	N	E	S
1♣	Dbl	1♠	2♡
Dbl			

Support Double for sure. North's takeout double does nothing to change the meaning of your double.

W	N	E	S
1♣	1◇	1♠	3◇
Dbl			

You have to draw the line somewhere. This double is not normally treated as support. When South bids two diamonds, the Support Double works well since you can stop at the two level. Over three diamonds, doubling to show three spades is not a safe action since you will be at the three level, which isn't a good idea if your side has a poor four-three fit.

However, I can see the merit of having double here still showing support and if so, you must have more than a minimum. Using the auction above, here are some examples to show Support Doubles at this level.

♠Q874 ♡KQ4 ◇Q73 ♣A83

Pass. Just not enough to bid at the three level. If you did bid three spades, it would show four trumps if using Support Doubles at this level.

♠KJ94 ♡A8 ◇543 ♣KQJ4

You would prefer to bid two spades but their bid took away that choice. In cases like this, you have to overbid a little in order to make sure your side does not lose its fit. This is a minimum three spade bid.

♠AQ74 ♡54 ◇A4 ♣AQ1084

Bid four spades. You would have jumped to three spades if given room to do so. With their taking away your jump raise, you have to bid a bit more aggressively than normal.

♠KJ3 ♡AK54 ◇73 ♣K863

Pass. This is a nice fourteen point hand with three good spades but it is not good enough to make a Support Double. It is one thing to play in a four-three fit at the two level and another to play in a four-three fit at the three level. You need more than this to make a Support Double, assuming you are using them at the three level.

♠KJ8 ♡AK73 ◇73 ♣AQJ3

Double, showing three spades. On hands where you are balanced, you will have a little more than an opening one notrump bid because with fifteen to seventeen high card point hands, you would have started with one notrump.

♠KJ8 ♡AQ74 ◇4 ♣AJ874

With shapely hands, you can double within this range. You need more than a minimum, remember, to be butting your head in at the three level when your side may be in a four-three fit.

A Summary of Support Doubles

If your partner responds one of a suit and your RHO bids anything less than two of your partner's suit a double by you is a Support Double no matter how the bidding has gone. If your RHO bids your partner's suit, a double by you is a Support

Double if their bid is a cue bid, and it is for takeout if it is a natural bid.

It is optional for your partnership to play Support Doubles through the three level too. Do not assume Support Doubles to be on at the three level unless you have specifically discussed it. The majority of players using Support Doubles only play them on through the two level.

How does responder continue bidding after opener's Support Double? What is forcing? What is not forcing?

When opener makes a Support Double, responder is expected to make a sensible decision. As far as I know, I have never seen anything published about how the bidding should go. When I played with an expert in a recent event, we had a simple Support Double auction which demonstrated that we needed agreements.

W	N	E	S
1♦	Pass	1♡	1♠
Dbl	Pass	2♣	

Do you have any idea what two clubs is? Is it forcing? Is it looking for the best contract? Are you obliged to go back to two hearts on all weak hands? For instance, does East have to bid two hearts with this hand?

♠843 ♡10873 ◇3 ♣KQJ83

East can imagine that clubs is a better place to play than hearts. At this point in the auction, East actually hates the idea of playing in hearts. How can you get to clubs? If two clubs is forcing, you can't get there. If two clubs is natural and passable, you can bid two clubs with some chance of it being the final contract.

Of course, when you have a better hand, you need a way to show it too. Take the following hand. What should you bid after partner makes a Support Double showing three hearts?

♠864 ♡AQ63 ◇74 ♣AQ94

Two clubs can't be right if that bid is used to show weak hands with long clubs. I will have a look at this hand in the following discussion.

W	N	E	S
1◇	Pass	1♡	1♠
Dbl	Pass	?	

Here is a list of what responder can do after the auction begins as shown. Most of the bids mean what you would expect them to mean. In some cases, though, the bids are tricky.

Pass   This is a rare action. It is possible you might pass the double for penalty, but I have never seen it happen.

1NT   One notrump is straightforward. It shows a spade stopper, six to ten points, and just four hearts.

♠KJ63 ♡9763 ◇J85 ♣Q9

With spades stopped, something in clubs, poor hearts, and no real reason to want to play diamonds, bidding notrump is best.

2♣   Bidding the unbid suit at the two level is not forcing when it is a minor suit. This is contrary to all general rules of bidding. You need a good five card or longer suit, no interest at all in playing in your four-three major fit, and a weak hand.

♠84 ♡J532 ◇83 ♣AQJ94

This is what two clubs looks like. You have too few points to be interested in constructive bidding and you don't like hearts. One notrump is not possible either. You will usually have a club suit like this one, but you could have a six card suit.

2◇   Going back to partner's suit is common. You show diamond support, deny interest in game, and imply four hearts. Both these hands bid two diamonds.

♠8643 ♡A863 ◇Q106 ♣J8

♠653 ♡KJ82 ◇8762 ♣A9

2♡   Watch out for this one. Two hearts is natural, but it does not promise five hearts. Responder may have to bid two hearts on a four card suit as a least-of-evils bid. If you are the opener, you must not get it into your head that partner has five hearts. Since there are other bids available to responder, the return to two hearts tends to show a decent suit, albeit possibly only four cards long.

♠963   ♡AJ87   ◇86   ♣J984

♠863   ♡J653   ◇83   ♣AKJ5

Responder has to bid two hearts with both of these hands. Fortunately, the second hand is rare.

♠J82   ♡J762   ◇63   ♣AQ73

Bid one notrump. The J82 of spades isn't a genuine stopper, but it is a lesser evil than bidding two hearts on J762.

2♠   Cue-bidding the opponents' suit is forcing to game. This is usually an exploratory bid with no specific goal in mind other than finding the best game contract.

Responder usually has just four of his major, but is allowed to have five or more. Opener will expect four until the message is further defined. Opener will bid notrump when he can and will do whatever seems best on other hands.

♠98   ♡KQ83   ◇J63   ♣AQJ3

Bid two spades. If partner can bid notrump, you will be happy to raise. If he can't, you will continue in some fashion. Until you hear your partner's next bid, you aren't sure where the hand is going.

♠864   ♡AQ63   ◇74   ♣AQ94

This is the hand I introduced a few pages ago. What to do with it? I would vote for two spades, a cue bid. We may have an easy game. We may play in three notrump, or we may end up playing game in a four-three heart fit.

♠763 ♡AQ84 ◊84 ♣KQ64

Here is a genuine problem. You do not quite have enough to
force to game. You might bid two notrump, not forcing, but
you are missing a spade stopper. My guess is to bid two hearts
on the theory that if partner has a minimum opener, he needs
around fifteen points to make three notrump worthwhile. He
did not open one notrump so looking for game is against the
odds. A tough hand!

2NT   Two notrump is invitational, as it is in most auctions. It
       promises four hearts, invitational values, and a stopper
       in their suit (spades).

♠K1074 ♡QJ73 ◊95 ♣AJ8

About right for the jump to two notrump. You could have a
point more if the hand is poor quality.

*You have another question to answer here. Opener can double or
redouble with a minimum twelve count, but he may have twenty
points and intend to bid again. If opener bids three diamonds
here, is it forcing, or is it weak? I suggest you play that it is
forcing.*

3♣   The jump to three of the unbid minor is a mystery bid.
       After much soul searching, I can see no obvious
       meaning. It can be used to show clubs and be either
       forcing or invitational. It can be used as an arbitrary
       slam try in hearts, possibly guaranteeing a singleton.

My guess, until I see proof to the contrary, is to play this bid as
a slam try in hearts promising five or more hearts so that
opener does not have to worry about having just three of them.

♠84 ♡AQJ87 ◊KQ7 ♣AJ5

Three clubs, if used as I describe here, tells partner that you
want to look for a slam. It is sort of a general purpose cue bid
announcing eighteen or more support points and inviting cue-
bidding from partner.

The difference between three clubs and two spades is that two spades is aimed at finding the best game contract, not aimed at exploring for slam.

3◇   This is a routine limit raise in diamonds. A jump in partner's minor shows eleven points, four hearts, and four or more card support.

♠875 ♡K873 ◇AJ73 ♣K2

You could have a jack more than this. Partner can pass or do whatever else he has in mind. Remember that his double did not limit his strength. He may have a big enough hand that slam is possible.

3♡   Just a game try in hearts showing five of them (or very rarely, an exceptional four). This is the equivalent of bidding three hearts over a raise by partner.

♠A104 ♡QJ873 ◇K104 ♣83

In support of hearts, this hand is worth around eleven points. Bid three hearts. West will know you have five hearts or a super four card suit and he will bid on or pass according to his strength.

3♠   Three spades, a jump cue bid, shows a stiff spade, good hearts, and slam interest.

♠3 ♡Q108763 ◇AK ♣KQ74

3NT   This is just what it sounds like. Responder wants to play in three notrump.

4♣,4◇ Both of these bids are splinters, just like three spades. They show a stiff, even in partner's suit, slam interest, and five or more trumps.

NOTE that if your LHO doubled one heart and partner redoubled, the bids would mean more or less the same as above. One distinction is that since LHO doubled as opposed to bidding one spade, you don't have a spade cue bid any more. Probably, you don't need it. If you have a good enough hand to

38

cue-bid, you can pass the redouble and try to double the opponents.

What if the auction is at the two level?

W	N	E	S
1◇	Pass	1♠	2♣
Dbl	Pass	?	

2◇　The return to opener's minor is just an offer to play there. It is not a strong bid and it does deny five spades. Opener will usually pass this bid unless he has a huge hand. Given that responder has four spades only, opener tends to avoid a spade contract.

2♡　Another curious bid. If responder really has hearts, he must have five spades. There is no need to play this bid as natural and non-forcing as was done with a new minor suit in the previous section. Two hearts, whatever it is, should be forcing.

REMEMBER that if East is able to bid a new MINOR at the two level, it is not forcing. It shows five or six cards and only four of the major. For instance:

W	N	E	S
1♡	Pass	1♠	2♣
Dbl	Pass	2◇	

This is not forcing, just suggesting diamonds as an alternative to spades.

♠Q763　♡8　◇KJ984　♣J43

Clearly, you would prefer to play in diamonds instead of spades if opener is willing to do that.

W	N	E	S
1◇	Pass	1♠	2♣
Dbl	Pass	?	

Continuing with the things that responder can do on the second round.

2♠   A return to two of the major is, as always, a weak bid. Responder can have four spades for this bid.

2NT   A game try showing eleven or so points, clubs stopped, and just four spades. Most notrump bids show about what you would expect.

3♣   The cue bid remains a game forcing call. I suggest that you do not make this bid if you can find a natural bid that will do. Cue-bidding is something to be avoided when possible.

3♢   The jump in opener's suit is still an invitational bid. Responder denies five spades.

3♡   Another strange bid. I think three hearts should be game forcing and show five-five in the majors.

3♠   A game try showing eleven points and five spades.

3NT   Just like it sounds. Responder wants to play in three notrump.

4♣,4♢   All three of these jump bids show singletons with slam
4♡   try strength. They also confirm spades as a good trump suit.

REMINDER   In competition, things are different when the Support Double is used instead of a raise.

W	N	E	S
1♢	Pass	1♠	Pass
2♠	Pass	3♢	

W	N	E	S
1♢	Pass	1♠	2♣
Dbl	3♣	3♢	

On the first auction three diamonds is forcing, an auction you should confirm with your partner. I have a history of stories where one partner thought it was forcing and the other thought it was an offer to play. I have personally two such stories where my partnership played in three diamonds, making seven. This is true and I can quote the hands, the partners, and the locations.

In the second auction, which includes some competitive bidding, three diamonds is not forcing. Opener can pass. From East's perspective, he might have a four-three spade fit and wish to play in diamonds. Three diamonds should be a competitive bid showing good diamonds, some points, and no interest in playing in spades. If East wants to make a game try in spades, use a three spade bid.

Normally, a jump to three spades would be a game try. In competition, you can't jump to three spades since you are already at the three level. Since you need a game try, saying that bidding three of the trump suit is a game try is the simplest way to achieve it. This is reasonable since you don't usually want to compete to the three level when you know partner has just three trumps.

When Responder Bids One Diamond Instead of One of a Major

W	N	E	S
1♣	Pass	1◇	1♡
Dbl			

When partner responds one diamond and RHO bids a major, there are some doubles you can use which are not strictly Support Doubles.

When partner responds one diamond and the next player overcalls with one heart, double by opener can be used to show four spades and three diamonds (maybe even four). If opener has spades and no diamond support, he just bids one spade. The same trick can be used after a two heart overcall, too. Double shows four spades and three card diamond support and more than a minimum opening bid.

When the opponents overcall one or two spades, you have fewer options. Against a one heart or two heart overcall, you can bid spades without increasing the level of the bidding. Spade overcalls are more difficult to contend with.

W	N	E	S
1♣	Pass	1♦	1♠
Dbl			

When the opponents overcall spades, it pushes the bidding up higher than you like. If they bid one spade, you have to go to the two level to bid hearts and if they bid two spades, you have to go to the three level to bid hearts. On the above auction, South overcalls one spade. A sensible use for double here is that it shows four hearts and says nothing about diamonds. You need a pretty good hand for this, but as long as you don't mind getting to the two level, you can double to show your hearts and not lose the suit. One benefit is that partner can go back to your original suit.

W	N	E	S
1♣	Pass	1♦	2♠
Dbl			

On this specific auction, you can double two spades to show four hearts just as you did after a one spade overcall. Be sure to have substantial extra points to cater to being at the three level. If you want to say that this double shows hearts and support for diamonds, you can't double when you have just hearts. I think your priority should be to show hearts. If you wish to play that this double shows support plus hearts, go ahead. The tradeoff is not huge.

Remember. If you double hearts, you show spades and diamond support. If you double spades, you show only hearts. If you like this treatment after a diamond response, be sure to remember that the trick applies only after a major suit overcall. It does not apply if they overcall one notrump.

A Quiz on Support Doubles

Regardless of whether you use Support Doubles, you should answer these questions to see what this convention is all about.

In the following auctions, what does West have for his last bid?

	W	N	E	S	
1.	1♣	1♡	1♠	2♡	
	Dbl				
2.	1♣	Pass	1♠	Dbl	
	Rdbl				
3.	1♣	1♡	2♢	2♡	
	Dbl				
4.	1♣	Dbl	1♠	2♡	
	Dbl				
5.	1♣	1♢	1♠	2♢	
	Dbl	Pass	2♠	Pass	
	3♣				
6.	1♣	Pass	1♠	1NT*	
	Dbl				*15-18
7.	1♣	Dbl	1♢	1♡	
	Dbl				
8.	1♢	1♡	1♠	2♢	
	Dbl				
9.	1♡	Pass	1♠	3♣	
	Dbl				

Answers

1.   West shows three card spade support. West's values are unknown. He can have from thirteen to twenty points.

2.   Redouble shows three card spade support. Just like the Support Double, the Support Redouble does not deny a big hand.

3.   Double is for penalty. Support Doubles only apply when partner bids a suit at the one level. Here, your partner's bid was two diamonds.

4.   Double shows three card spade support. It does not matter that both opponents are bidding. Opener can have any range of values.

5.   Three clubs shows a big hand. His double showed three card support and now his three club bid shows extra values. It is not forcing, though. NOTE that East may have just four spades.

6.   Double can be support showing three spades or it can be played as penalty. I like using it as a Support Double. It is reasonable, AND it avoids your having to remember exceptions. A hidden gain for this bid is that your partner may be able to pass for penalty. If you have a minimum hand, you do not have to double. Some judgment is needed with Support Doubles.

7.   This is one of the optional trick auctions. This double promises three card diamond support AND four cards in spades. West may have a big hand.

8.   The two diamond bid probably shows a heart fit for North. It is better to use double to tell East about three card spade support than to show good diamonds. If opener has a big hand, he will follow with another bid.

9.   Most partnerships that play Support Doubles define this double as penalty. Make sure that your partnership has a precise agreement on this. Support Doubles can turn on you in a bad way if you do not have firm agreements.

In the following auctions, what does East's last bid mean? In some sequences there is more than one possible bid for East. On the first sequence, for example, you are asked to define what 2♣, 2♦, or 2♡ would mean by East on the second round.

1.
W	N	E	S
1♦	Pass	1♡	1♠
Dbl	Pass	2♣/2♦/2♡	

2.
W	N	E	S
1♡	Pass	1♠	2♣
Dbl	Pass	2♦/2♡	
		2♠/2NT/3♣	

3.
W	N	E	S
1♦	Pass	1♡	1♠
2♡	Pass	3♦/3♡	

4.
W	N	E	S
1♣	Pass	1♦	1♠
Dbl	Pass	2♡/3♣	

5.
W	N	E	S
1♣	1♦	1♡	1♠
Dbl	Pass	2♣/3♠	

6.
W	N	E	S
1♦	Dbl	1♡	2♠
Dbl	Pass	3♦	

7.
W	N	E	S
1♦	Pass	1♡	1♠
Pass	Pass	2♡	

Answers

1. **2♣** is not forcing. East has four hearts and five or more clubs.

    2♦ is a diamond preference (bad hearts).

    2♡ is a weak bid. East may have four hearts and no other bid.

45

2.   2◇   is natural and not forcing.

          2♡   suggests a doubleton heart and only four spades.

          2♠   can be bid on four or more spades. It is a weak bid. As you can see from the previous sentence, East is not always obliged to bid a four card spade suit. He can show a doubleton heart if he wishes.

        2NT shows game try points with clubs stopped and only four spades.

          3♣   a cue bid, usually shows a balanced hand. It is game forcing.

3.   3◇   is forcing and is a search for game. When your side has an eight card major suit fit, you no longer need ways to play in opener's minor suit.

          3♡   is a game try. East probably has five hearts, although this is not a certainty.

4.   West's double showed four hearts and the ability to compete at the two level; it is not a Support Double. East's 2♡ bid just shows four hearts.

          3♣   is a limit raise. West can bid on or pass it.

5.   2♣   is just club support. East has to bid, remember, so he may have bid with a crummy hand.

          3♠   is a splinter bid showing five or more hearts and a stiff spade. East has slam try points for this bid, or else he would just bid four hearts and not give unnecessary information to the opponents.

6.   Since South's two spade bid is higher than two of responder's suit (hearts) West's double is for penalty. East is saying he has a weak hand with no defense and lots of diamond support.

7.   East's two heart bid is somewhat forward-going. West did not make a support bid of any kind so does not have three card support. East must have six of them. Also, since East could have passed one spade, East must have some values. Eight or nine points is likely.

What does opener's final bid mean in these auctions?

1.
	W	N	E	S
	1♢	P	1♡	1♠
	Dbl	Pass	2♡	Pass
	2NT			

2.
	W	N	E	S
	1♢	P	1♡	1♠
	Dbl	Pass	2♣	Pass
	2♠			

3.
	W	N	E	S
	1♢	P	1♠	2♡
	Dbl	Pass	2♠	Pass
	3♢			

4.
	W	N	E	S
	1♢	P	1♠	2♣
	Dbl	Pass	3♠	Pass
	4♣			

Answers

1.   West showed he has three card heart support and on the next round he showed he has eighteen or nineteen points with spades stopped.

♠K104 ♡AJ3 ♢AKJ87 ♣Q9

East knows that West has a good hand along with three card heart support. If West bid two notrump directly over one spade, he would show the same values but with only two hearts.

♠K104 ♡AJ ♢AKJ87 ♣Q97

2.   A lot is happening here. East's two club bid is weak showing four hearts and a minimum hand. West showed three hearts and when East showed clubs, West finally admitted to having a big hand. West's likely hand is nineteen or so points without a spade stopper, looking for three notrump.

♠763 ♡AQ8 ◇AKQJ8 ♣K6

This hand should show heart support by using the Support Double. The two spade bid usually shows something like this hand.

3.　　　West has spade support and a strong hand with nice diamonds. Three diamonds is a strong bid but passable if East has a minimum.

♠QJ3 ♡32 ◇AKJ1086 ♣AJ

This is on the minimum side for this sequence. Basically, West is showing a hand that wanted to jump to three diamonds and has stopped along the way to show three card spade support.

Interestingly, if you are using Support Doubles, you can bid some hands better when the opponents compete than when they are quiet. This is usually not the case.

4.　　　West showed his spade support and East made an invitational jump. East ought to have five spades and eleven points for this bid. East expects that West has a normal opening bid at this stage and is asking if opener has a maximum. West, on this hand, has much more and judges that a slam may be makeable opposite East's invitational hand. His cue bid says that. Here is a possible West hand for this bidding sequence.

♠AQ10 ♡83 ◇AQJ83 ♣AJ8

If East has the right eleven points, slam is possible. The four club bid is how West can find out without arbitrarily bludgeoning the bidding too high.

One Last Question — a Very Important One

W	N	E	S
1◇	Pass	1♡	2♣
Pass	Pass	Dbl	

What does East's double mean?

Do you play Negative Doubles? If you do, you know all about those hands where responder wants to double an overcall for penalties and has to pass to let opener make a double. The same principle applies here.

W	N	E	S
1◇	Pass	1♡	2♣
?			

♠AJ10 ♡3 ◇AK874 ♣KJ96

Say both sides are vulnerable. West would love to whack two clubs and collect whatever is coming; but if West is using Support Doubles, he can't double two clubs. In the same way that Negative Doubles force you to pass and hope your partner can double, Support Doubles do the same thing. With this hand you have to pass and pray that your partner can double.

What does your partner need to double? He needs a hand that would be happy to defend two clubs, doubled, if you had made a penalty double. Here are a few hands that your partner can have.

♠Q873 ♡AQ984 ◇J9 ♣82

East can double with this. East knows among other things that West does not have three hearts, because he did not make a Support Double. With North passing, it is logical, or at least plausible, that West wanted to make a penalty double and could not because of system.

♠Q73 ♡KJ642 ◇3 ♣Q853

East should not double, because West can't possibly have a club stack. West rates to have some kind of minimum opening bid that was not able to rebid over two clubs. East should pass and expect to set two clubs a trick or two.

♠KQ43 ♡Q986 ◇QJ63 ♣5

Your singleton club suggests your partner has good clubs but your hand is very favorable for diamonds. It is best, probably,

to bid three diamonds, a limit raise. This follows the excellent
guideline that when you have a good fit, you should not rush to
defend. This choice may cost you a spade fit. West could have
four spades. If you miss a spade fit, you can justifiably feel
injured by their two club overcall.

MAXIMAL DOUBLES

It used to be that players did not bid as much as they do today.

W	N	E	S
1♠	Pass	2♠	3♡
3♠			

Twenty years ago, West's three spade bid meant that he was
interested in game. If West were not interested in game, he had
to pass. Bidding three spades just for the sake of competing
was not done. The idea was that bidding and going down was
bad bridge. Better to let the opponents have the hand in three
hearts.

Today, the value of a partscore is better known. It is not good
bridge to pass three hearts, if you have anything that suggests
three spades may make. There are many hands that West might
bid three spades with as long as he was comfortable that East
would not take it seriously and bid four.

The trouble was that West was only allowed one meaning for
the three spade bid. Either it was invitational or it was
competitive. Science has finally found a way for West to have it
both ways. The invention of the Maximal Double gives West an
extra option. It works this way.

W	N	E	S
1♠	Pass	2♠	3♡
?			

When the opponents bid the suit just below the suit you are
bidding and raising, you double when you have a game try
hand and you bid three of your suit when you wish to compete.

♠AK973 ♡873 ◇AQ7 ♣A3

You wish to invite a game. Double is the way you do that.

♠AQ10652 ♡32 ◇K7 ♣K43

With a sixth spade, you would like to bid three spades as a competitive bid and not as a game try bid. Using Maximal Doubles, this three spade bid is competitive, NOT invitational.

Do you use Maximal Doubles on ALL auctions where they bid the suit below your suit?

W	N	E	S
1♠	Pass	2♠	3♡
?			

W	N	E	S
1♠	2♡	2♠	3♡
?			

W	N	E	S
1♠	Dbl	2♠	3♡
?			

In the first auction, South came in with three hearts all by himself. It is quite possible that you would like to double them for penalty. Do you want to give up the penalty double here or do you want to use a Maximal Double?

In the second auction, North and South have a fit. It is not likely that you want to double them for penalty. Giving up a penalty double when they have a fit is a modest loss.

In the third auction, North made a takeout double and South bid hearts. It is reasonable to assume they have a fit, in which case doubling for penalty won't get you rich.

I suggest (and play with most of my partners) that when the opponents have a fit, the double is a Maximal Double, showing game try values. However, when the opponents do not have a fit (as in the first sequence), I play the double as penalty. This combination is not perfect, because it gives you problems when you have a hand like the first one in this section. Here it is again. You open one spade.

♠AK973 ♡873 ◇AQ7 ♣A3

If North overcalls two hearts and your partner raises and South bids three hearts, you can use the Maximal Double as a game try. If North doubles one spade and your partner raises and South bids three hearts, you can use the Maximal Double as your game try. However, if North passes and your partner raises and South bids three hearts on his own, a double would be for penalty and three spades would be a game try.

If you do not like exceptions, then play Maximal Doubles on all sequences where they take away your bidding room. You will have some successes and some frustrating moments but you will have fewer 'forgets'.

The opponents' bidding does not always take away your bidding room. Note the following three auctions.

W	N	E	S
1♠	Pass	2♠	3◇
?			

W	N	E	S
1♠	2♡	2♠	3♣
?			

W	N	E	S
1♠	Dbl	2♠	3♣
?			

In the first and second sequences, South is bidding his suit on his own. In the third sequence, South is responding to a takeout double so he has a fit. Still, *because you have room to make a game try*, a double is for penalty.

In the first sequence, you can bid three hearts as a game try. In the second and third sequences, you can bid three diamonds OR three hearts as a game try. Even if the suit you bid is a cue bid, you rate to have some length there. Not to worry. This one almost never comes up.

BE AWARE – When you have only one suit to bid as a game try, you will sometimes have to bid a suit that is not a classic game try suit. Ideally, when you bid a new suit as a game try, you have something like Q984 or K1065. You bid a suit where help in partner's hand will be appreciated.

W	N	E	S
1♠	2◊	2♠	3◊
?			

On this bidding sequence, the only game try bid you have is three hearts. When this is the case, your game try seldom has any relevance to the suit you bid.

♠AKJ73 ♡74 ◊J4 ♣AK105

A three heart bid by you tells your partner that you are interested in game, but it does not promise that you have a heart suit. This is a flaw in the methods.

When you have room for more than one game try, your bid tends to be an honest evaluation of your hand and your partner will tend to like high cards in the game try suit.

W	N	E	S
1♠	Dbl	2♠	3♣
?			

♠AQ962 ♡AKQ ◊Q108 ♣62

With this hand, your game try should be three diamonds, telling your partner that you would like diamond help.

W	N	E	S
1♠	Pass	2♠	3♣
?			

♠A10963 ♡A3 ◇QJ ♣K1074

Double for penalty. You could bid three diamonds or three
hearts as a game try. However with four clubs, you have good
defensive possibilities and can express your opinion by
doubling.

W	N	E	S
1♠	Dbl	2♠	3♡
?			

♠J10973 ♡AKJ9 ◇A2 ♣Q6

Be aware that a double by you is a game try double. It is not
for penalty. They have a fit and they are bidding the suit just
under your suit. The rule, if using Maximal Doubles in the way
I suggested, is that this double is a game try and says nothing
about hearts. There are rare moments like this one where you
can't double for penalty because of your system. It happens.

Both Sides Can Use Maximal Doubles

W	N	E	S
			1♡
1♠	2♡	2♠	3♡
?			

There is no reason why West cannot use a Maximal Double
here. South is competing, not bidding strongly. At this moment,
it is easy to imagine West's having a game try. If you are in
agreement, Maximal Doubles will work for you here too. The
normal restraints apply. If West has no room to make a game
try, a double becomes artificial, not for penalty.

54

Other Auctions Are Possible with Proper Discussion

W	N	E	S
		1♣	Pass
1♠	2♡	2♠	3♡
?			

♠K10643 ♡87 ◇A6 ♣QJ83

West wishes on this hand to make a game try. If he had a weaker hand with better shape, he might wish to compete to three spades. If your partnership is comfortable with Maximal Doubles, you can extend them to auctions like this one too.

W	N	E	S
1♣	1♠	2♣	2♠
?			

♠4 ♡AJ3 ◇KJ32 ♣AQ983

West starts with one club and is quite pleased to hear East's raise, a normal bid showing seven to nine support points. Since East is raising a minor suit, he rates to have four card support and could have five.

If South had passed, West would have made a forcing trial bid of two diamonds, looking for more information from East. With South's raise to two spades getting in the way, West has an awkward choice. He would like to make a strong noise here. What should that be?

West can bid three diamonds, risking ending up in a poor four club contract if East has the wrong cards. He can bid three hearts, too, with the same risks. West might even bid three spades, although I am not sure that East would know what it means.

I suggest a double. This is defined as showing this approximate shape and enough points that game is possible. You rate to have a singleton in their suit because with a stronger but balanced hand, you might have opened with one notrump. There are lots of hands your partner can have where game is laydown. There are also some hands where three clubs is high enough. Double lets you do it all.

♠J752 ♡Q72 ◇97 ♣KJ104

Facing this hand, three clubs is enough. On a bad day it might go down.

♠9652 ♡K4 ◇Q76 ♣K762

This hand, with three fitting high cards, makes five clubs a fine contract. It isn't cold but it is certainly worth bidding.

♠876 ♡62 ◇AQ7 ♣J10642

You won't bid to six clubs, but it could make. This is an odd hand. If the defenders lead hearts early on, you could make six, or you could make four.

The rules for this double are easy enough. It applies only when there was an overcall and a raise with your partner raising your minor in between their bids. Opener says he has a singleton in their suit. Opener might have a huge hand with a doubleton, but the hand with a singleton is normal. Opener says he has enough to try for game. This description is quite accurate and your partner ought to be able to decide what to do.

Whatever decision he makes rates to be a good one. If opener has more than this hand, he can bid again later, thus indicating that he has more than a minimum double.

W	N	E	S
1♣	1♡	3♣	3♡
Dbl			

At the three level, this double is for penalty. You are welcome to play it is a game try, as per the earlier discussion. Nothing wrong with that. Without discussion, though, this double should be for business.

NEGATIVE DOUBLES AFTER A NOTRUMP OPENING

Your partner opens one or two notrump and your RHO overcalls. All kinds of conventions, such as Lebensohl, Rubensohl, Stolen Bid, and a few others, are in use to combat this situation. Among them should be included the Negative Double.

After a One Notrump Opening Bid

W	N	E	S
1NT	2♣	?	

W	N	E	S
1NT	2◇	?	

W	N	E	S
1NT	2♡	?	

W	N	E	S
1NT	2♠	?	

Against all of these auctions you can play Negative Doubles, and you can add Lebensohl if you wish against two diamonds, two hearts, and two spades. Here is a normal enough hand to show you how this works.

W	N	E	S
1NT	2♣	?	

Two clubs can mean a multitude of things today. I have seen it show one of the following at various times during my career: the majors, any one-suited hand, clubs, clubs and any higher ranking suit, hearts and a minor, clubs and both majors, diamonds. It goes on. Here is your hand.

♠Q1074 ♡K4 ◇AJ43 ♣763

If North had passed, you would have bid Stayman looking for a spade fit. North's two club bid got in your way. Now, what should you do? A very simple answer is to play that double is

Stayman, and two diamonds and two hearts are transfers. When you choose any of these three bids, the bidding continues exactly as if North had not bid two clubs.

Regardless of what you choose to do against overcalls of two diamonds or higher, I strongly suggest you use a double of two clubs as Stayman in conjunction with Jacoby Transfers.

W	N	E	S
1NT	2◇	?	

The higher their overcall, the less you can do with it. It is very acceptable to play a double here as Stayman, but you do not have any transfer bids.

Some players use a convention called Stolen Bid. They use double to replace the artificial bid that was "stolen" by their opponent's overcall. Stolen Bidders would double the two diamond overcall here to show they wanted to transfer to hearts. This is not a good convention. Take the auction here where your RHO overcalled two diamonds. Using double as Negative lets you explore for both majors. Using Stolen Bid lets you explore for just one. Keeping both majors in the picture is more important than keeping just one.

If you use double to show a Stayman type hand you can just bid the suit when you have a long major. There may be some moments where Stolen Bid has merit but this is not one of them.

What Do You Need to Double?

Keep in mind that if you make a Negative Double of a two level overcall, your partner may have to bid two notrump if he cannot bid a major suit. This means you must have at least the values to be safe at two notrump.

If your RHO overcalls two diamonds, natural, you would double with this hand, ♠KQ87 ♡J873 ◇32 ♣Q82, which is a minimum for the bid. You intend to pass whatever partner bids.

♠73 ♡A63 ◇QJ83 ♣QJ63

Pass or bid three notrump. You can't double for penalty if you use Negative Doubles. The best you can do, if you want to play for penalty, is to pass and hope your partner reopens with a double. He will do this if he has a hand with short diamonds and acceptable shape for a takeout double. One example.

W	N	E	S
		1NT	2♡
Pass	Pass	?	

♠A83 ♡J3 ◇AQ94 ♣AJ74

East has shortness in hearts. Assuming you are using Negative Doubles, he can reopen with a double hoping that you have a heart stack. In fact, he can double with this hand even if you are not using Negative Doubles, hoping to find you with a useful minimum hand. If you are playing Negative Doubles, the onus for opener to reopen is stronger than normal.

If They Overcall at the Three Level

When an opponent is able to bid at the three level, your problems are greater yet. Take this ordinary hand.

♠Q874 ♡J1073 ◇32 ♣AQ6

Your partner bids one notrump and your RHO bids three diamonds. What a mess. You can double for penalty but with two small diamonds, this is not a hot solution. You can bid four diamonds to ask for a major suit, but if partner does not have a major, you are at the four level without a parachute. Finally, you can opt for three notrump. Could work. But if partner has a major suit and four of a major is your contract, your three notrump bid may not be best.

A sensible solution is to extend Negative Doubles to the three level. You need enough points to be safe at this level, and you need proper shape for the bid. Other than that, judgment should see you through. Please note that if you double, your partner can pass if he has strength in their suit. You may yet get a penalty out of this.

For the sake of partnership agreements, I suggest that a new suit at the three level be competitive. Opener can pass but he is allowed to bid again too. His choice. If you have a game forcing hand, start with a double and then bid your suit if appropriate.

This suggestion will help you on many hands, and it gives you an understanding that is workable. If you bid three hearts over three diamonds and your partner has no idea what you mean, you are in trouble. One of my most quoted mantras is that a pair that has decent agreements and plays them well is better off than a pair that plays the best system in the world and forgets half of it.

W	N	E	S
1NT	3◇	?	

♠QJ863　♡43　◇A652　♣92

Bid three spades. Your partner can pass, raise, or bid three notrump. Hopefully it will all work out.

♠AQ764　♡K84　◇73　♣Q73

Double and guess what to do next. If your partner bids hearts, bid three spades, forcing. If he bids three spades, be grateful and raise to game. If he bids three notrump, guess between passing and four spades. Passing is reasonable. If he bids four clubs, bid four spades. At least you and partner will be on the same wavelength.

Finally, if you find that you do not like your opponents bidding at the three level, remember your frustration and return the favor when you have a weak hand with a long suit and they are the ones opening one notrump. Oh, yes. Check the vulnerability before getting too frisky.

NOTE – I suggested that if you bid a suit, it is not forcing. I know of many players who insist that bidding a suit is forcing. This works fine with my usual caveat being that you must have agreements.

After a Two Notrump Opening Bid

W	N	E	S
2NT	3◇	?	

You won't run into many opponents with enough nerve to bid over a strong two notrump opening bid, but it can happen. You will find that they are never vulnerable when they do and for some reason, you usually are. It is easy to see why their bidding can hurt you. You have something like this.

♠A763 ♡Q874 ◇87 ♣J62

You want to show the majors but how do you do it? A sensible treatment is to say that double is for takeout, something like Stayman, and any suit bid is natural and forcing to game. With the hand here, you would double to ask partner to bid a major.

♠843 ♡KJ873 ◇43 ♣Q94

Bid three hearts. You cannot have a Stayman bid and a transfer bid too. The best you can do is to bid three hearts and let partner choose a game contract.

♠873 ♡732 ◇Q864 ♣A87

You can probably set three diamonds four tricks but it is hard to double them if your double is used as Stayman. Best is to bid three notrump.

NOTE that you do not lose all chances of setting them a bundle. If you make a Stayman double, your partner may choose to convert your double to penalty by passing. If this happens, you get a penalty that you could not get in any other way.

After They Overcall Your Strong 2♣ Bid

You open with two clubs, your big opening bid, and your LHO somehow manages to find a two spade overcall. Do you know what a double by your partner means? Is it penalty, showing:

♠KJ843 ♡543 ◇J4 ♣1084

Or is it something else?

There are at least three sensible meanings for double and they all have merit. They are:

1.   Double is penalty.

2.   Double is a random noise saying that your partner has four or more points. This is called a Positive Point Double.

3.   Double is a random noise saying that your partner is broke. This is called a Negative Point Double.

If Double is for Penalty

Briefly, if you play the double is for penalty, the most common meaning for double, you will do all right when you can collect a penalty. Nothing wrong with that. However, you must be careful that when you double, you do not have a hand that might be useful for slam.

♠KJ843 ♡543 ◇J4 ♣1084

This is the hand I showed earlier. Doubling for penalty makes perfect sense. You expect to set two spades a lot, and you do not expect that your hand will be worth much to your partner if he plays the hand.

♠AJ954 ♡K74 ◇QJ4 ♣74

Let's say you are vulnerable and they are not. If you have this hand, you can double two spades and you will get a very nice penalty, guaranteed. However, your hand is so good that your side probably has a slam, perhaps even a grand slam. If so, you have to set two spades seven tricks to come out ahead. Down six will be worth 1400 and your slam will be worth more than that.

If You Use Double to Show Points

In this case, you double on hands worth four points or more. Some players think a king that is not in the overcalled suit is enough. Using this double, you double when you have a smattering of values and no interest in playing for penalties.

♠73   ♡J83   ◇K873   ♣J432

This is not a beautiful hand but facing a two club bid, you rate to have a game. By doubling, you tell partner you are not broke. This double is forcing to game, which is nice in that you don't have to worry that one of your later bids might be passed out.

If You Use Double to Show a Bad Hand

♠873   ♡107653   ◇43   ♣J83

This is a bad hand. The way you show a bad hand is to double. This warns your partner that you have nothing so he won't be optimistic. You need to agree that if your partner bids a suit, it is forcing. Your partner may have a two-suited hand that requires more than one bid to describe it. On sequences where your partner bids his suit twice, you can certainly pass. This brings up a can of worms.

W	N	E	S
		2♣	2♠
Dbl	Pass	3♡	Pass
?			

♠653   ♡3   ◇96543   ♣J743

What should you bid with this? A possible treatment is to play that the cheapest bid is artificial, saying you have a horrible hand with a misfit. If you had two hearts you could raise to four hearts, but with this hand, you really hate to do that. Better to bid three spades as a warning.

Fortunately, this scenario won't come up that often. If the overcall is two hearts or two diamonds, your partner will sometimes be able to bid at the two level, which gives your side more bidding room.

If You Use Positive or Negative Point Doubles, How Do You Penalize Their Overcall?

W	N	E	S
		2♣	2♠
?			

♠KJ843　♡543　◇J4　♣1084

♠AJ954　♡K74　◇Q84　♣74

If you have the first hand, you would like to play for penalty. The way to get that result, assuming you play either Positive or Negative Point Doubles, is to pass and wait for your partner's bid. If he doubles (for takeout), you will pass, of course, and get your penalty. Your partner will not double unless he has a hand that is willing to play for penalties. If he has a 5-4-3-1 hand, he will tend to double. If he has a long suit and strong shape, he will bid naturally.

With the second hand, I suggest you bid two notrump over two spades, showing values and a stopper, saying you have a hand that does not want to defend two spades, doubled. Your intent is to follow your two notrump bid with some strong bidding.

I have a much longer discussion of this bidding area in my *CONVENTIONS* software. It has 1600 pages of text so has more room for discussion and examples than I do here.

DOUBLES BY THE SIDE THAT COMPETES

There is a long list of doubles that can be used by the side that enters the bidding after an opening bid. The list covered here is not nearly as long as it could have been.

SNAPDRAGON DOUBLE

A popular, but not too effective, double is the colorfully named Snapdragon Double. If nothing else, it adds a conversation piece to your convention card. The definition is simple enough. When your partner overcalls and RHO bids a new suit, a double by you shows five decent cards in the unbid suit and a doubleton in your partner's suit. For example.

W	N	E	S
	1♣	1♡	1♠
Dbl			

♠10974 ♡J9 ◇AKJ74 ♣52

This is about par. You have enough values to compete, and you wish to give partner as many options as possible.

How high should you use this convention? Does it apply when your RHO bids a new suit at the two level? Does it apply after partner overcalls at the two level? These questions need to be answered. My suggestion is that Snapdragon Doubles only be used if the bidding is still at the one level.

This is a useful convention, but it seems to me that its frequency is low. Telling your partner about your two card support seldom leads to much. And getting partner to bid your long suit is also not a high frequency occurrence. There is one nice aspect to this convention, however, and that is if your partner is on lead, he has good information about what to lead.

W	N	E	S
	1♣	1◇	1♡
Dbl			

This sequence lends itself to a small added touch. Double can be used to show four spades and three diamonds. With five spades you just bid them. This is the one auction that lets you bid your suit at the one level so this added distinction is conveniently available.

This next double actually has two different names. They refer to the same thing.

EXTENDED SNAPDRAGON DOUBLE
EXTENDED RESPONSIVE DOUBLE

Assuming that Snapdragon Doubles are useful, there is an extended family of doubles that are similar. Some of them are very useful. These are based on one easy assumption. When they open the bidding and your partner enters the bidding by doubling or overcalling, your side almost never doubles them for penalty at the one level. If you agree with this, then it is not hard to agree that penalty doubles are not worth keeping, especially if something better can be found. Here is a worthwhile alternative. Use doubles as takeout.

W	N	E	S
1♣	1♡	1♠	Dbl

In the same way that South's double can be used as Snapdragon, showing a tolerance for hearts plus the unbid suit, almost all the other one level doubles can be defined in some useful manner.

Can you remember the last time your partner overcalled at the one level and you doubled your RHO's bid for penalty and set it a lot?

W	N	E	S
1♣	1♠	1NT	Dbl

W	N	E	S
1◇	1♡	1♠	Dbl

Have either of these sequences occurred lately? How about this one? Do you remember setting your opponents on this auction?

W	N	E	S
1♣	Dbl	1NT	Dbl

You just do not get rich doubling one notrump on this sequence.

Why is this? The answer is actually easy to see. When your LHO opens, he has his twelve or thirteen points. When your partner overcalls or doubles, your RHO needs eight or nine points to bid one notrump. He will have them if he is playing sane bridge. This means that your side has less than half of the high card points. Here is an example which demonstrates this theme. It is based on one of the sequences shown above.

W	N	E	S
1♣	1♡	1NT	?

♠Q873 ♡84 ◇A1076 ♣KQ3

Your partner overcalls one heart and your RHO bids one notrump. You have this rather flat hand. Should you double one notrump for penalty? I think not. Here is the complete hand.

```
            ♠ K9
            ♡ AQ1063
            ◇ 983
            ♣972
♠ AJ52                      ♠ 1064
♡ 95                        ♡ KJ72
◇ Q54                       ◇ KJ2
♣AJ86                       ♣1054
            ♠ Q873
            ♡ 84
            ◇ A1076
            ♣KQ3
```

Look at what is happening here.

1.   When they bid one notrump, it always turns out that
they have half of the deck or more. If you have a good hand, *it
means that your partner has a minimum hand.*

2.   When your RHO bids one notrump, it shows, among
other things, that he has a stopper or stoppers in your partner's
suit. It may be hard for you to set up tricks there. On this hand,
East has a fairly normal one notrump bid. Try as you may, you
are not going to set one notrump. If you are careless and if
declarer guesses well, he may be able to make one or two
overtricks.

Here is another example.

W	N	E	S
1◇	1♡	1♠	?

♠AQJ73 ♡4 ◇KQ83 ♣873

You can probably set one spade but why double the bid? One
spade is forcing. Doubling a forcing bid is a losing proposition
for sure. All that happens is that you give the opponents
information before they are entitled to learn it. Since the one
spade bid is forcing, the auction is sure to continue. You may
have a second chance to double if the auction goes well for you
and that will be at a higher level than it is now.

If you give up penalty doubles at the one level what should the meaning be?

In all cases save one, a double by you is for takeout. What it is takeout for is the tougher question. Here are some example auctions and suggestions.

W	N	E	S
1◇	1♡	1♠	Dbl

This double is Snapdragon, showing a tolerance for partner's hearts and a club suit. This convention was covered a few pages ago.

W	N	E	S
1◇	1♡	1NT	Dbl

This double is different. It cannot be Snapdragon because there are two unbid suits. Your partner won't know which suit you are showing. This double shows the two unbid suits, as in the following hand.

♠Q10763 ♡4 ◇32 ♣AQJ83

You really do not want to give up. If your partner has three cards in either of your suits, you can contest the bidding safely. If you don't have a tool available to show your hand, you have to guess between bidding one of your suits or passing. Don't guess, use the double.

W	N	E	S
1♣	Dbl	1♡	Dbl

This double can be played in two ways. I present both in my order of preference.

Double is for penalty. If you choose this option, it will be the only penalty double you have at the one level following a bid from your partner and a bid from your RHO. You show four hearts exactly and at least eight high card points. Well, maybe a great seven high card points will do. Having exactly four hearts is much more important.

♠A7 ♡QJ83 ◇J1074 ♣983

Your double does a number of things. It may expose a psych by East or it may allow you to arrive in a playable fit even if East really does have four hearts. It will cause the opponents to run, and then you will be better able to judge the auction. When this happens, your side can get to a heart contract if your partner wishes to bid them. If he has four hearts, he is allowed to bid hearts naturally, knowing you have four of them and some high card values.

♠A7 ♡QJ832 ◇J1074 ♣92

The correct bid with this hand is an eye-opening two hearts. This is a natural bid, promising FIVE or more hearts and around eight or nine points. With five hearts and more points, you jump to three hearts or bid game. This treatment puts pressure on your partner to remember the convention and it also demands that he have the proper shape for his takeout doubles. Given that these things exist, this agreement is an excellent one to have.

Alternatively, double of RHO's bid is takeout, promising the two unbid suits. This is an effort to play in the right suit in case partner does not have four cards in both suits.

W	N	E	S
1♣	Dbl	1♡	Dbl

♠J873 ♡K43 ◇K1084 ♣84

You have enough to bid with but you might be nervous about bidding spades for fear that diamonds are a better fit. You can use double here as takeout for the two unbid suits. If you double, you promise seven or so points. Do not double with less. NOTE that the bidding may continue and if so, your partner will have to decide whether to bid on.

What if East bids 1NT?

This one is tricky. On this sequence, there are three unbid suits for you to bid. There is a lot of potential information for you to give to your partner.

When the opening bid is not one spade, here is a possible treatment. Assume you have enough points that you feel like bidding.

W	N	E	S
1◊	Dbl	1NT	?

Double with the two lower unbid suits.

♠87 ♡Q1097 ◊32 ♣A9852

Opposite a takeout double, you have a good enough hand to compete. Whether you should compete in hearts or clubs is not clear. Doubling and getting an opinion from your partner should clear things up. NOTE that you do not rate to have a five card major when you make this bid. With a five card major, you should just bid the suit.

Cue-bid opener's suit with the two higher unbid suits.

W	N	E	S
1♣	Dbl	1NT	?

♠KJ62 ♡J965 ◊Q62 ♣J10

Bid two clubs. This hand has sufficient values to be in the bidding too, but which suit to bid is a problem. If you use a cue bid to ask for the majors, you can handle this hand.

W	N	E	S
1♡	Dbl	1NT	?

♠Q874 ♡10764 ◊AJ73 ♣4

Bid two hearts. This shows the two higher unbid suits, spades and diamonds. This way you get both suits into the picture. You could bid two spades but by bidding two hearts, you keep both suits in the picture without losing bidding room. NOTE that you do not have to make this cue bid when holding spades and diamonds. It is optional.

♠KQJ8 ♡874 ◇J764 ♣62

With this hand, you know spades are OK. Just bid two spades.

♠K953 ♡763 ◇43 ♣A1085

Bid two spades. Double would show the minors and two hearts would show spades and diamonds. Bidding two spades is hardly a disaster because that is what you would normally do without having these special doubles to help you.

W	N	E	S
1♠	Dbl	1NT	?

When the opening bid is one spade, it is a good idea to switch the meanings of the bids. Use the following schedule of bids instead.

Double with hearts and a minor. Since hearts is the most important suit here, you want to get it into the bidding as cheaply as possible.

♠K432 ♡Q873 ◇3 ♣QJ83

Double. This shows four hearts and one of the minors. If your partner has only three hearts and has four-four in the minors, he will bid two clubs. You will pass with clubs or bid diamonds with diamonds. Should opener rebid two spades, your partner can bid two notrump to ask for your minor suit, if he wishes to compete. Similarly, he can bid hearts knowing you have exactly four of them.

♠A874 ♡Q974 ◇Q73 ♣82

With only hearts, just bid them. Partner usually has four hearts, although he does not promise them. With this hand you can barely afford to bid two hearts. This bid does not promise five hearts, as you can see. Remember that this denies holding a minor suit.

♠8743 ♡4 ◊KJ83 ♣QJ106

Cue-bid with both minors. If your partner's doubles are sound enough that you don't mind being at the three level, bid two spades. This will find your fit. NOTE that your partner won't expect much from you. If you have a very good hand, most unlikely on the bidding, you will have to follow up with a strong bid. If you have both minors and do not want to be at the three level, just bid your better minor.

♠9763 ♡3 ◊KQ107 ♣J764

Bid two diamonds. This hand is not good enough to be competing at the three level.

♠873 ♡32 ◊QJ983 ♣K87

Bid two diamonds. This is good enough to compete over one notrump.

♠873 ♡3 ◊QJ983 ♣K872

Bid two diamonds OR bid two spades. One benefit of bidding two diamonds is that you may get to stop at the two level. You do not have to use the cue bid. That is a function of judgment.

NOTE that when your RHO bids one notrump, he tends to have real points. Your side almost never has a game contract. For the most part, you are fighting for a partscore. Winning these little wars is very important, something that is known to anyone who has lost an event by one or two points.

FINAL THOUGHT - Conventions have a way of growing more than you want them to. You may notice that in the structure shown above, there is no meaning assigned to two notrump. Some players would say that enough is enough and that no meaning is needed. Some players, however, cannot get enough of a good thing. If you are one of those players, you may wish to add something special for two notrump. Perhaps it should show five-five in the minors. Perhaps it should show a six card minor and four hearts. There are all kinds of things you can create if you like to build things. Feel free to add if you wish.

Rosenkranz Double (and Redouble)

W	N	E	S
	1♣	1♡	1♠
?			

♠A874 ♡1074 ◇KJ4 ♣643

♠9863 ♡A104 ◇KJ4 ♣643

Holding either of these hands, you would like to raise hearts. Using normal methods, you would just bid two hearts and whatever happens, happens.

Some of the time when you raise, you end up on lead, but often opener will buy the hand and your partner will lead a heart. How do you feel if he leads the six of hearts?

On the first hand, with the 1074 of hearts, I know how I would feel. It means my partner has led away from a broken heart holding such as the KJ862, and the opponents are going to benefit from the lead. On the second hand, with the A104 of hearts, the lead is fine and most of the time it works out OK.

The Rosenkranz Double addresses this issue. The way it works is for West to double when he has a heart raise with a high honor (ace, king, or queen) and to bid two hearts when he has no high honor.

Similarly, if your RHO makes a Negative Double of your partner's overcall, you can play that a raise shows no honor and a redouble promises an honor. This convention definitely has its moments. It has some serious minuses too.

It is easier for the opponents to judge when to bid notrump when the location of the high honors in hearts is known. Sometimes when you double, opener can make a two level rebid when a raise would have gotten in his way. And finally, you may rarely suffer a penalty double when the opponents can judge that their trump honors are well placed.

Here is a list of issues you need to discuss with your partner.

1.   Do you ever break system and make a double with just honor-doubleton? If you do, your partner won't know whether he should compete further for fear that you may have just a doubleton trump.

2.   Do you use the raise to show the honor or the double to show the honor? Some players like to reverse the meanings from the original form and if so, your partnership better know it.

3.   Do you use Rosenkranz Doubles only when your RHO bids a new suit or even when your RHO raises or bids one notrump?

You will notice that you cannot use Snapdragon Doubles and Rosenkranz Doubles. They conflict with each other. Also, as you will see, if you decide to use Responsive Doubles, you cannot use Rosenkranz Doubles when the opponents bid and raise a suit over partner's overcall.

In a nutshell, Rosenkranz Doubles are never the only possible meaning for a double. There are other meanings for doubles, no matter what the auction, where you might wish to be doing something else. Always consider whether you are losing more than you gain by choosing to use these doubles. Does all of this commentary mean that Rosenkranz Doubles do not work? Not at all. There will be many hands where your side makes a good decision on opening leads that would not be available without Rosenkranz Doubles.

Lawrence Double

Having flirted with Rosenkranz Doubles and not always being happy, I was bothered. Fortunately, a hand came along that made me consider them in a more narrow vein. This was the hand that got my attention.

♠K10986 ♡84 ♢AQ84 ♣93

W	N	E	S
	1♣	Pass	1♡
1♠	2♡	2♠	3♡
Pass	Pass	Pass	

A spade lead felt fine on the bidding and I did that. Sadly, my partner had raised on J52 and my lead was the only one to give away the contract.

This got me to mulling over my choice and eventually a light went on. Why not use Rosenkranz Doubles on this auction? If my partner would double with a raise that included a high honor (Ace, King, or Queen) and raise when he did not have an honor, I would know what to lead with this hand.

The reason this double seems to work is that it occurs on one auction only. Your LHO opens and your RHO bids a new suit. After your overcall, whether at the one or two level, opener raises. When all these factors are in place, the raise and the double can be used to show an honor or lack of an honor. Not only that, if their side is using Support Doubles and makes one, you can use a redouble and a raise to the same effect.

I like this treatment because for once, there is no other useful meaning for a double that conflicts with it. This double does not exist for most players. Here is a partial list of auctions where this double applies.

W	N	E	S
	1♣	Pass	1♡
1♠	2♡	?	

W	N	E	S
	1♣	Pass	1♠
2◇	2♠	?	

W	N	E	S
	1♡	Pass	2♣
2◇	3♣	?	

W	N	E	S	
	1♡	Pass	1♠	
2◇	Dbl*	?		*Support

In the first three auctions there is no current meaning for double that makes much sense. You can't want to double for penalty, and given you did not bid over the opening bid, you do not rate to have a good suit to introduce at this time. Using the double and the raise to separate honor raises and non-honor raises makes sense to me because this is one sequence where the overcaller rates to be on lead.

On the last auction, the same considerations apply. Using redouble and the raise to show honors or no honors is also useful because you (West) will be on lead much of the time.

Is this a proven convention? I think so because it does something useful, and it does not get in the way of any other treatment that might be more useful. Here is one interesting success.

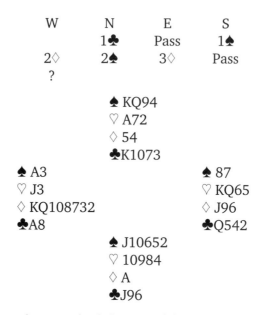

W	N	E	S
	1♣	Pass	1♠
2♢	2♠	3♢	Pass
?			

♠ KQ94
♡ A72
♢ 54
♣K1073

♠ A3
♡ J3
♢ KQ108732
♣A8

♠ 87
♡ KQ65
♢ J96
♣Q542

♠ J10652
♡ 10984
♢ A
♣J96

If West knew that East had the ace of diamonds, he would bid three notrump. East's three diamond bid denies an honor so West knows that he does not have nine fast tricks. What West should bid is not perfectly clear, but he is comfortably able to reject three notrump as a possibility.

ACTION DOUBLES

I am not at all sure what to call this family of doubles or what it takes to qualify. What I can do is give you some examples of doubles that clearly are not for penalty, but which classically might have been interpreted in that way. Here are some examples along with observations. You are sitting West with no one vulnerable.

W	N	E	S
	1♣	Dbl	1♡
1♠	2♡	Pass	Pass
?			

♠KJ63 ♡43 ♢A852 ♣652

Your hand is maximum for your one spade bid. You can, if you wish, compete further. The way to do this is to double. You do not have hearts, but you are not expected to. Double says that you have a maximum one spade bid and probably only four spades. Your partner can pass and play for penalty, if he feels that is best, or bid two spades if he prefers that. East will play you for eight or nine points and four spades and that is what you have.

Just as on most Action Double sequences, your hand does not have any trump tricks. The double shows maximum points for the bidding so far.

W	N	E	S
	1♣	Pass	2♣
Dbl	Pass	2♡	Pass
Pass	3♣	Pass	Pass
?			

♠AQ93 ♡A93 ◇AQJ6 ♣52

Double. You already made a takeout double of two clubs, and the bidding clearly says you can't have a club stack. At this point in the bidding you are pretty sure the hand belongs to you but it is not clear what the best continuation is. Double says you have a solid hand and want to go on. Your partner is instructed to make the winning bid. (Isn't it nice how you can pass the buck?) Your partner knows you have only three hearts or else you would just raise so his bid, whatever it is, should be accurate. He can pass if he has a balanced hand with three clubs. He can bid three hearts if he has five of them. He can bid another suit if he has one. Hopefully, your high cards will see you through whatever decision your partner makes.

W	N	E	S
		1◇	Pass
1NT	2♣	Pass	Pass
?			

♠K103 ♡73 ◇Q63 ♣A9863

Another case where you can't have good trumps but you do
have a maximum hand. Double is reasonable. Your partner
knows you don't have four spades and that your hand is limited
by the one notrump bid.

W	N	E	S
		1◇	Pass
1♡	1♠	Pass	Pass
?			

♠72 ♡AJ832 ◇J4 ♣K1065

This hand is related to Support Doubles. If using Support
Doubles, your partner denies as many as three hearts. When
your partner fails to make a Support Double and the opponents
compete and go nowhere, you should stop and think. Where
are the points? Where are (in this case) the spades?

It is likely that your partner has spades and wanted to make a
penalty double but could not, because it would be a Support
Double. You can (and should) double. You have enough points
to compete. And, you do not rate to have a lot of spades.
Typically, you have a hand that has nine or more points and no
obvious distributional message to offer.

Another way of looking at this is to ask yourself this question. If
your partner had made a penalty double, would you have been
happy to sit for it? This hand passes this test. If East had
doubled one spade for penalty, you would have been happy to
pass.

W	N	E	S
		1◇	Pass
1♡	1♠	Pass	2♠
?			

♠72 ♡AJ832 ◇Q4 ♣K1065

This setup looks a little like the previous one. In this case, you have one additional point, and your RHO just raised to two spades instead of passing. Your double is still takeout oriented. Your partner is less likely to pass, but he rates to have enough shape that this bid will work well for you.

W	N	E	S	
		1♠	Pass	
1NT*	2♡	Pass	3♡	
?				*Forcing

♠103 ♡43 ◇AJ98 ♣AJ752

Double. Again, a decent hand that does not have a clear bid. This is not penalty, but it shows a maximum for your previous action. Partner will usually take it out, but if he passes, you are content.

W	N	E	S
		1♠	Pass
2♣	2◇	Pass	Pass
?			

♠42 ♡AQ7 ◇963 ♣AK1073

Double. You might have a diamond stack but this hand is more likely. You have a good hand with no clear bid. Doubling is a way to say that you do not have a natural bid available that you are happy with. Considering that your partner did not rebid spades, did not show four hearts, and did not raise clubs, he rates to have some diamonds, which means that declarer is in trouble. He will get some diamond tricks but not much else.

Action Doubles can be defined as doubles that are takeout oriented, but which are often left in. In most cases you will have defined your hand's point range and now are saying that you have a maximum and do not want to give up.

The following is an example of a hand that does not fall into the Action category.

W	N	E	S
2♡	2♠	Pass	Pass
?			

♠2 ♡AJ10975 ◇K83 ♣Q105

You started with a normal two heart bid and North overcalled with two spades, after which the bidding came to a halt. *How can this be?*

I would not be content with the bidding so far and would double two spades. This is a takeout double stating that I have a maximum hand plus my shape is as good as might be expected. It is clearly defined as takeout although West harbors the wish that East can pass. Here is the complete hand.

```
                    ♠ AQ986
                    ♡ K86
                    ◇ AJ
                    ♣J84
    ♠ 2                              ♠ KJ1074
    ♡ AJ10975                        ♡ 42
    ◇ K83                            ◇ Q97
    ♣Q105                            ♣K73
                    ♠ 53
                    ♡ Q3
                    ◇ 106542
                    ♣A962
```

Two spades doubled by North went down three after less than ideal dummy play. It was always down two, however, and that would also have been a good result. Since making three hearts is the limit of the hand, a two trick penalty will be a top or close to it.

Why didn't East double two spades? It would be a bit greedy. His hand, good as it is for defending against spades, is not worth much should the opponents run to another contract. It is even possible that two spades will make when West has a minimum weak two heart bid. East is willing to pass for penalty after West's double, because West shows both a maximum weak two bid and some additional defense.

NOTE that West essentially made a balancing bid. This is not a true Action Double. On this hand East chose to sit for the double, but with a different kind of hand, he would have bid. Give East either of these hands, for instance.

♠Q873 ♡4 ◇AQ964 ♣J76

East would bid three diamonds, fully expecting West to have three card support.

♠Q874 ♡Q8 ◇QJ74 ♣K73

East would bid three hearts. He couldn't raise the first time because he had little to offer. But when West doubled two spades, East was faced with a different kind of decision. Passing could be wrong; there is an excellent chance that it makes. Against that East knows that his values are working for hearts since West should have short spades, length in the minors and a maximum. Certainly, three hearts looks to be a better contract than two spades, doubled.

RESPONSIVE DOUBLE

In some ways, the Responsive Double is related to the Negative Double. Both exist in order to help you out in competitive auctions. These doubles are intended to let you bid with hands which have the strength to bid but do not have an obvious bid to make.

One main difference between these two doubles is that the Negative Double is used by the side that opened the bidding, whereas the Responsive Double is used by the side that is competing. The Responsive Double works in two ways.

W	N	E	S
	1♡	Dbl	2♡
Dbl			

W	N	E	S
	1♡	1♠	2♡
Dbl			

When your partner makes a takeout double and your RHO raises, you will often be interested in competing. This is a situation where it pays to be aggressive, so you should be alert to any opportunity to bid. If you have a suit to bid, you can bid it. Sometimes, though, you have a hand worth bidding, but with no clear choice of what to bid. Perhaps you have two poor suits to choose from. Some of the time when you have two suits to show, you can use the Responsive Double to do that.

Here are some questions and guidelines for Responsive Doubles after partner makes a takeout double.

1.   The Responsive Double is used only when RHO raises opener's suit. If RHO bids a new suit, Responsive Doubles are off.

2.   If the opponents are bidding a MINOR suit, a Responsive Double shows both majors. If you only have one major, bid it.

W	N	E	S
	1◇	Dbl	2◇
?			

♠Q964 ♡83 ◇AJ3 ♣10873

You have a comfortable two spade bid. There is no reason to show the clubs. Partner has asked you for a major suit and you have one. Since a Responsive Double shows both majors, this hand does not qualify.

♠Q964 ♡J1074 ◊832 ♣A7

On this hand you have the same values, but you have both majors. Partner could have three of one and four of the other, so you would like to bid the right one. The way to do this is to use the Responsive Double. Double asks partner to bid his better major.

3.   If the opponents are bidding a MAJOR suit, a Responsive Double shows both minors. With only the other major or only one minor, you would bid the suit.

4.   Your partnership must decide how high to play Responsive Doubles. That is, if RHO raises to the three or four level, is the Responsive Double still on?

When your partner makes a takeout double, you can usually tell when there is a fit. If you have two suits to offer, you are almost guaranteed a fit. For this reason, if you have the values to bid, you should feel safe in making a Responsive Double up to the level of four diamonds.

5.   Your partnership must decide whether to play Responsive Doubles when the opening bid is a weak two or a weak three bid and partner doubles.

W	N	E	S
	2◊	Dbl	3◊
?			

W	N	E	S
	3◊	Dbl	4◊
?			

Would double be Responsive on either or both of these auctions? Definitely. When you have two suits, you can count on there being a fit so looking for it is a good idea. NOTE that when your partner doubles a preempt he promises a little more than when he doubles a one bid. You may adjust your bids to cater to that. You will find that this is a very important and versatile tool.

85

W	N	E	S
	1◇	Dbl	2◇
?			

♠AJ74 ♡10874 ◇74 ♣J73

Not much, but enough to double. You show the majors and enough points to compete at the two level. Notice how much happier you are by letting partner choose the suit. If you guessed to bid two hearts, you would hate seeing KQ62 of spades and Q92 of hearts in the dummy. Could happen. Conversely, if you guessed to bid two spades you would not enjoy finding dummy with the 1082 of spades and the AQJ5 of hearts.

W	N	E	S
	1♣	Dbl	2♣
?			

♠AQ42 ♡KJ74 ◇J9 ♣873

Double. A double is not limited. Here, your partner will bid a major and you will raise to the three level. Your partner will judge whether to continue. This hand is about as good as you will have on this auction.

W	N	E	S
	1♠	Dbl	2♠
?			

♠732 ♡J7 ◇A1093 ♣QJ63

Double. When they are bidding a major suit, your double shows the minor suits. This is a minimum hand since your partner has to go to the three level to bid.

W	N	E	S
	1♠	Dbl	2♠
?			

♠J63 ♡Q872 ◇AQ104 ♣97

Bid three hearts. A double would show the minors. Some partnerships use a double followed by three hearts to show a weak three heart bid and a direct three heart bid to show sound values, but assuming you are not using this treatment, you have to bid three hearts when you have them.

W	N	E	S
	1◇	Dbl	3◇
?			

♠QJ73 ♡K1094 ◇763 ♣K3

Double. You show eight or more good points and both majors. If your partner bids three hearts or spades, you have a close decision to bid again or to pass. I would vote for pass but have sympathy for you if you go on.

W	N	E	S
	1♡	Dbl	3♡
?			

♠652 ♡8 ◇AJ873 ♣KQ97

Double. As the bidding gets higher, you need better values. Your partner has to bid a minor at the four level, so you'd better come through with a nice hand.

W	N	E	S
	1◇	Dbl	4◇
?			

♠KQ72 ♡Q876 ◇7 ♣KJ63

Likewise, enough to double four diamonds, looking for a major suit fit at the four level. It is much safer to ask partner's opinion than to choose yourself. The takeout double does not promise two four card majors but it generally promises one. Playing in the proper trump suit is worth a lot. There is one nice extra to this choice. You are showing a decent hand with both majors. If your partner wishes to, he can pass and play for penalties. This would be unexpected, but it is possible.

W	N	E	S
	1♡	Dbl	4♡
?			

♠Q73 ♡43 ◊AJ873 ♣K109

Double. This auction is higher than four diamonds so double is no longer Responsive. It is akin to the Action Double discussed earlier. Your double just says you have high cards and instructs partner to do something good. In general he will pass your double, but if he has a very shapely hand, he is allowed to bid something. He will not, however, count on you for both minors, merely high cards along the lines of what you have here.

When your partner overcalls and your RHO raises, you have sensible choices of conventions to use. You can use Responsive Doubles, discussed here, or you can use Trump Raise Doubles, which will be discussed in the next section.

If you have a decent hand with the two unbid suits, you can use Responsive Doubles to handle an assortment of hands that would be hard to bid with otherwise.

W	N	E	S
	1♣	1♠	2♣
Dbl			

In this example, West is showing hearts and diamonds and enough points to be comfortable competing.

RULES and guidelines for Responsive Doubles after partner overcalls and they raise.

1.   The Responsive Double applies ONLY when they open the bidding and RAISE. Be aware that Responsive Doubles are off if partner overcalls and RHO bids a new suit. If you double on this auction, your double falls into another category (see discussion of Snapdragon Doubles).

2.   A Responsive Double tends to imply 5-5 shape with enough points that you are comfortable competing. If you have

extra points, you can fudge a little when you have 5-4 shape and your four card suit is good. If your partner has room to bid at the two level, you need a nice eight points; but if he must go to the three level, you need about ten.

3.   A Responsive Double denies trump support for partner's overcall. Raising partner should be your first priority.

4.   When partner overcalls and your RHO raises, you do not have the same expectancy for a fit that you do when your partner makes a takeout double. You have to bid more gingerly in your efforts to find a fit.

W	N	E	S
	1♣	1♠	2♣
Dbl			

♠9 ♡KQJ9 ◇A10532 ♣J86

West has a good enough hand to compete, but it's not clear whether to bid hearts or diamonds. Either suit could be right. Double asks partner to choose. Your five-four distribution is slightly unexpected. When you have this shape, you have to have extra values. You would not double without the queen of hearts, for example.

♠32 ♡QJ832 ◇KQ754 ♣5

This hand has fewer points that the first hand, but it has better shape. There is little doubt that West would like to get into the auction, but as with all two-suited hands, the problem is to ensure getting to the best suit. The Responsive Double helps here. NOTE that your partner can bid at the two level. Be aware that you may strike out, even with this five-five shape. Give your partner this hand.

♠KQ864 ♡94 ◇102 ♣AJ76

Your partner has a nice overcall but your side does not have a fit, which means your double can get you in trouble. A worthwhile try but not guaranteed to work.

Let's make one point clear. When your partner doubles, you do not have to guess whether your side has a fit. You know the suits your partner is showing and you know if you have a fit. If your partner overcalls, you do not know if your side has a fit. Your partner might have just one or two little cards in each of the unbid suits as in the last example.

When you have five-five in the unbid suits you can hope for a fit but you cannot count on a fit. This means you have be cautious. This is an area where there are diverse opinions. I suggest that you play Responsive Doubles *after partner's overcall* up to three diamonds. My reasons for this include many factors, one of which is that your side may be able to stop at the three level. Feel free, if you have a strong opinion, to use a different range here.

NOTE that if you decide to use them only up to three diamonds, you will not have room to use them after a weak two heart or two spade bid by the opponents.

W	N	E	S
	2♡	3◇	3♡
?			

South's three heart bid is higher than my suggested level.

As I noted earlier, finding a fit after partner's overcall is more unlikely than finding a fit after partner makes a takeout double. This is why I suggest playing Responsive Doubles to the four diamond level after a takeout double but only to the three diamond level after an overcall.

You do lose the very unimportant penalty double but that is small potatoes. When your LHO opens and your RHO raises, it is doubtful that there will be a hand where you want to double them. You gain being able to find your best fit, a huge benefit, plus once in awhile your partner will be able to pass your double for penalty.

Before rushing to add these to your convention card, read the next section for a very sensible alternative.

CUE-BID DOUBLE

Responsive Doubles after partner overcalls are useful, but they do not seem to come up as often as Responsive Doubles after partner makes a takeout double. This is because you need a shapelier hand and better values to make a Responsive Double after an overcall than you do after a takeout double.

Jeff Rubens wrote a series on various doubles back in 1968 in *The Bridge World* in which he introduced many new ideas. One of his treatments is something he called a Cue-bid Double. It works like this.

W	N	E	S
	1◇	1♡	2◇
?			

If you are using Responsive Doubles, a double by West would show spades and clubs, a perfectly satisfactory treatment. If you are using Cue-bid Doubles, this double is used to say that you had intended to cue-bid two diamonds in support of partner's overcall suit, hearts. Here is the kind of hand that it was invented for.

W	N	E	S
	1◇	1♡	2◇
?			

♠J73 ♡Q83 ◇63 ♣AKJ83

You want to raise hearts, but you do not want to get to the three level to do it. If South had passed, you would have cue-bid two diamonds and rested in two hearts if East showed a minimum overcall. South's raise took away your cue bid so if you wish to show a good raise, you have to cue-bid three diamonds or perhaps use some other artificial means to show a good hand.

Jeff felt that if you compared the number of times that a Responsive Double would be used with the number of times that a Cue-bid Double would be used, the odds would favor using the Cue-bid Double. If you like this treatment, you have to go further and decide how high to play it.

W	N	E	S
	1♡	2♣	2♡
?			

Should this Cue-bid Double be used after a two level overcall too?

W	N	E	S
	1◇	1♡	3◇
?			

How about after your RHO jump raises? If you have a normal raise of seven to nine points, it is easy to bid three hearts over South's three diamond bid, but if you have an eleven or twelve point raise you will be awkwardly placed. Hands like these two can drive you nuts when you do not have a way to sort them out.

♠J6 ♡K732 ◇932 ♣K1094

♠K3 ♡KQ6 ◇873 ♣QJ542

Should you bid three hearts with both of these hands? The Cue-bid Double handles the second hand, and lets you bid three hearts with the first hand. Your partner has a better chance of doing the right thing when you use this combination.

BALANCING DOUBLES

This topic is actually more in the family of takeout doubles but I am asked enough questions about it that I will offer a few thoughts here. For much more detail, refer to my book, *The Complete Book on Balancing*.

Since balancing doubles come up in so many situations and since one rule won't cover all of them, I will just offer up a number of examples and see what can be deduced from them.

Let's assume no one is vulnerable in these hands.

W	N	E	S
	1♣	Pass	Pass
?			

♠AJ87 ♡Q984 ♢QJ4 ♣84

Double. When reopening against a passed out one bid, you can double with as little as a king less than you need for an immediate double. You are not trying to compete in the normal meaning of the word. In the balancing seat, you also have the goal of stopping them from buying the hand cheaply.

W	N	E	S
			1♡
Pass	2♡	Pass	Pass
?			

♠Q1073 ♡83 ♢A83 ♣Q1097

Double. When the opponents have a fit, they are in a contract that they like. If you let the opponents play in a contract that they like, you will usually get a poor result. Your double is aimed at buying the hand, hopefully making, but often down a small number, OR nudging the opponents a trick higher where you have a better chance of setting them.

W	N	E	S
			1♢
Pass	1NT	Pass	Pass
?			

♠73 ♡KQ6 ♢AQ108 ♣QJ106

Double. Using double as penalty is a wise idea. When the opponents stop in one notrump, it is usually unwise to balance. They have not found a fit so you do not rate to have a good fit either. On this hand, they are trying to make seven tricks with limited values. You know their diamond suit is not working, so they won't have an easy time getting tricks.

W	N	E	S
	2♡	Pass	Pass
?			

♠K874 ♡A3 ◇J1074 ♣KJ8

This is an OK balancing double of two hearts. It is not entirely safe to balance against a preempt because the bidding is a level higher than after a one bid, plus you know that suits will divide worse than normal. When you reopen with a double after a weak two bid, you can have a little bit less than a normal double, but not much. If you had a singleton heart here, you might double with eleven high card points.

W	N	E	S
	2♡	Pass	3♡
?			

♠QJ87 ♡3 ◇K1074 ♣A874

North made a weak two bid and South raised. If you pass, LHO will also pass and your partner will have a decision. It is OK for you to double now. This is not a full value double because you are effectively balancing. When you know that the auction is about to end, you can double for takeout on less than normal values, even though you technically are not in the reopening seat.

W	N	E	S
	1NT	Pass	2♣
Pass	2♡	Pass	Pass
?			

♠10973 ♡3 ◇QJ105 ♣AJ104

They seem to have run out of steam. Even though opener has a good hand, responder has not promised anything. He might have a weak hand and be hoping to escape from one notrump. You can double this for takeout, relying on your partner to remember there is an opening one notrump bid out there.

Assorted Other Doubles

Doubles When They Cue-bid a Suit Your Side Has Bid

1. Your partner overcalls, and you double an immediate cue bid.

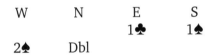

W	N	E	S
		1♣	1♠
2♠	Dbl		

This is a common situation. One of the bidding tricks used by almost everyone is to play that a cue bid of an overcall shows a good hand, usually with a fit for opener. Some players play that this shows a limit raise or better. Some players play that it shows a fit and is forcing to game. In either case, the cue bid shows a good hand. You will find an occasional opponent who cue-bids for no reason at all, but even these opponents promise values.

Whatever the cue bid means, a double by you should have a purpose. That purpose should not be an ego-strutting exercise in being heard. It should contribute to the auction and not just be a random noise.

A very useful meaning is to play that a double says you would have raised to two spades had you been able to. If you use this bid, you will be able to show a normal raise without having to bid to the three level. You should not make this bid with trash since the purpose of your bid is to help your partner decide whether to bid again.

Usually you will have a normal raise with just three card support. An honor will help. Here is the auction again.

W	N	E	S
	1♣	1♠	2♠
?			

♠763 ♡QJ763 ◇QJ4 ♣64

Best to pass. You have bad spades and not much shape.

♠Q84 ♡KJ84 ◇43 ♣8732

This is an OK double. You have a spade honor and some potentially useful cards in hearts.

♠J873 ♡A73 ◇J83 ♣1094

You might double with this hand too. It has four trumps and a nice high card, however it also has poor shape and minimum values. Normally, you do not double with four trumps.

♠QJ98 ♡A874 ◇874 ♣43

With four trumps and a prime card, it is probably best to bid three spades. You have enough that three spades should be safe. Remember that their cue bid shows values, and that suggests your partner has a minimum overcall. You do not want to offer him up as a sacrifice.

♠K3 ♡J9873 ◇Q843 ♣43

Pass. Double on this sequence shows real support, not just an honor.

2.   Your partner overcalls, and you double an immediate
       splinter bid.

W	N	E	S
	1♡	1♠	3♠
Dbl			

This one is easy. You are telling your partner that you have a
hand that is willing to have him bid four spades, most likely as
a sacrifice. You won't have a big hand, but you do have
something.

♠J873 ♡873 ◇K984 ♣84

Bidding four spades with this, no matter what the vulnerability,
would be too much. You do not mind telling partner that he is
welcome to do so if he wishes. He has been warned by the
three spade bid that trumps will break poorly and will take that
into consideration.

3.   You overcall and double an immediate cue bid by
       opener.

W	N	E	S
			1♣
1♠	2♣	Pass	2♠
Dbl			

Doubling is foolish without a reason. Doubling to show good
spades gains little; your partner will lead a spade after your
overcall anyway. What it does do is give the opponents an extra
round of bidding, which they may be able to use.

What should double mean? One good treatment is to say that
you have a good playing hand and are willing to compete but
need something from your partner to make it effective.

♠AQJ874 ♡43 ◇KJ108 ♣3

This hand is willing to go higher, but with a little help from
partner. East could have three spades to the king and nothing
else. He might also have four spades and a useful card like the

queen of diamonds. Either of these hands would pass over two clubs and would know from your double that it was right to bid three spades later. Bidding three or four spades all by yourself is wrong since your partner might contribute a singleton spade or a hand with nothing useful or both.

4.   Your partner overcalls, and you double a delayed cue bid.

W	N	E	S
			1♡
1♠	2♢	Pass	3♢
Pass	3♣	?	

This situation is less common but it has enough importance that you should use this suggestion. Your partner bid one spade; everyone at the table knows that three spades will not make, nor will it be the final contract. Your double should have a purpose.

East's double promises one of the top three spade honors and at least a doubleton. East did not bid over North's two diamond bid, so he can't have real spade support, but he may have a good enough spade holding that he would like a spade lead. Here is a hand to show how this kind of thing works.

```
                      ♠ 94
                      ♡ K2
                      ◇ AJ953
                      ♣KQ92
  ♠ KJ763                          ♠ Q82
  ♡ 6                              ♡ 109753
  ◇ 42                             ◇ Q107
  ♣AJ863                           ♣75
                      ♠ A105
                      ♡ AQJ84
                      ◇ K86
                      ♣104
```

W	N	E	S
			1♡
1♠	2♢	Pass	3♢
Pass	3♠	Dbl	

East passes over two diamonds, probably the right thing to do with this mess. Later when North bids three spades, tentatively asking for notrump, East doubles to say he has a spade honor. If South bids three notrump, West knows to lead a spade, not a club, and three notrump is down. If West does not get help from East during the bidding, he may well lead a club and that results in ten tricks for declarer.

This double is very important. If you (or your partner) use it wisely, it means that when you DO have an honor in partner's suit, you can double to show it. When you DO NOT have an honor in partner's suit, you can PASS to deny it. Negative inferences from this will help your partnership in more ways than one.

5.   You open and your LHO overcalls. Your RHO cue-bids your suit and you double.

W	N	E	S
1♢	1♠	Pass	2♢
Dbl			

This situation is very common. The most common meaning is to say that you have good diamonds and want a diamond lead. But is that really a good idea? I think not. Your partner is going to lead a diamond almost all of the time. It is, after all, the suit you opened. It should not be necessary to double if all you want is a diamond lead. You should get that anyway.

Of additional importance is that when you double, you give them an extra bid to help sort out what they are going to do. There are better uses for this double and you should use one of them. Here are two good treatments.

i.   Use a double to tell your partner that you were thinking of competing to three of your suit.

♠8 ♡KJ4 ◇AQ8753 ♣A105

If your partner has a little support, he can show it.

♠9764 ♡Q763 ◇J104 ♣J3

This is a lousy hand but since you did not bid the first round, partner will not expect much. He said he was willing to compete, and what you have is pretty good under the circumstances. Bid three diamonds if you have room to do so.

ii.   Use a double to show a takeout double of their suit. One of the nice things about this double is that if your partner has nothing to bid, he can pass. There is no way they are going to play it in two diamonds, doubled. One of the opponents will go back to spades. West can double two diamonds with this hand.

♠2 ♡KJ84 ◇AKJ76 ♣K104

It is true that you can pass the cue bid and later double two spades if possible, but that won't happen if the opponents can get the bidding to the three level. Incidentally, if you have a better hand than this one, you can double two diamonds and then double two spades also.

Both of these treatments are better than using double to say you want a diamond lead.

DON'T-LEAD-ME DOUBLE

This double might fit into the previous section but it is so different that I am giving it a place of its own.

W	N	E	S
			1◇
1♠	3◇	Pass	3♠
Dbl			

♠Q86543 ♡AKJ3 ◇3 ♣104

It looks like they may end in three notrump and if so, your partner is going to be on lead. That will probably result in a spade lead and that is exactly what you do not want. The Don't-Lead-Me Double helps here. You can double to say that you do not like this suit and really wish partner would lead something else. On this hand, your partner will have to choose between clubs and hearts, but his hand should probably tell him what you wish.

Here is a real life example. With both sides vulnerable, a lot of bids were found by everyone, especially East.

```
                    ♠ AQJ6
                    ♡ Q9762
                    ◇ A5
                    ♣A9
    ♠ K1053                      ♠ 984
    ♡ J4                         ♡ 10
    ◇ K42                        ◇ J10987
    ♣KQ73                        ♣J842
                    ♠ 72
                    ♡ AK853
                    ◇ Q63
                    ♣1065
```

W	N	E	S
1◇	Dbl	2♣	2♡
3♣	3◇	Dbl	4♣
Pass	4◇	Pass	5♡
Pass	6♡	Pass	Pass
Pass			

The auction needs some footnotes. I wish I could provide them. The one diamond bid was part of a forcing club system. The double was standard. The two club bid was (I believe) both minors. Two hearts was natural and conservative. The three club bid was natural. The three diamond bid was a cue bid. The double was a Don't-Lead-Me Double (I believe). The rest of the auction was interesting, and the final contract was six hearts.

David Bird wrote up the play of this hand in his book, *Bridge Squeezes for Everyone*. South made six hearts by squeezing West out of his long spades and the king of diamonds. It would have been even easier if West had led a diamond, which he might have done without the warning double from East.

Use this double with care. Be warned that there are complications with this double. If you double them at too low a level, they may decide to redouble and play it there. Not likely but quite expensive if they do. Especially, you must be sure that your partner won't confuse the Don't-Lead-Me Double with some other conventional double your side may be using. Say the bidding goes this way.

W	N	E	S
1◇	1♡	Pass	2◇
Dbl			

In another section of this book I discuss three possible meanings for double. It may be used to say that you have good diamonds and want the suit led, that you are showing a takeout double of their hearts, or that you have a good hand and are willing to hear partner compete to three diamonds.

If you have agreed on one of these, you had better not suddenly try a Don't-Lead-Me Double. Your partner won't have as flexible a mind as you, and the result will be bad. Trust me.

Without going into extensive example auctions, I think I can safely say that the Don't-Lead-Me Double occurs when you double a cue bid on an auction where you might wish the lead of this suit AND where you have no other agreements about the double.

DOUBLES OF CUE BIDS WHEN THEY ARE LOOKING FOR A SLAM

W	N	E	S
			1♠
Pass	2◊	Pass	2♠
Pass	3♣	Pass	4♣
?			

♠74 ♡J1074 ◊763 ♣KJ109

The opponents used a two over one sequence to find their spade fit and then started looking for a slam. Should West double?

The answer is no. West is going to be on lead whenever South plays in spades and that is likely to be what happens. Why tell South all about your clubs? Let him find out what you have in clubs during the play, not during the bidding.

This time you are East.

W	N	E	S
			1♠
Pass	3♠	Pass	4♣
Pass	4♡	?	

♠94 ♡KQJ7 ◊8764 ♣J74

With this hand you desperately want a heart lead. From your perspective, the only lead you care for at all is hearts, and if you pass, your partner is likely to look elsewhere. You would hate a diamond lead, nor would you care for a club lead. Double and help partner.

♠874 ♡QJ108 ◊7532 ♣Q8

You don't have as strong an urge for a heart lead here, but you would still hate a diamond lead, a likely choice from West's point of view. Since North promised the ace of hearts, there is no combination of hearts where a heart lead will be a bad choice and it actually might be a killing choice if your partner has the king of hearts. Double is fine with this hand. Do not overdo doubling with this suit quality. Be sure that partner's lead of this suit will not cost a trick.

Here is another auction for comparison.

♠874 ♡QJ108 ◇7532 ♣Q8

W	N	E	S
			1♠
Pass	2◇	Pass	3♠
Pass	4♠	Pass	4NT
Pass	5♡	?	

You could double five hearts, but this may cause your partner to lead the ace of hearts if he has it. Since this is possible, you should not double. Who knows? A club lead might be best, and you do not want to tout West away from that lead.

DOUBLES OF GAME TRIES

This is more of a reminder than anything else. If your opponents make a game try, and you feel like doubling it, be sure your partner is on lead. If you are on lead, do not advertise your hand.

W	N	E	S
			1♡
Pass	2♡	Pass	3◇
?			

♠QJ8 ♡87 ◇KJ754 ♣J94

Absolutely never double a game try by opener no matter how good your holding is in their game-try suit. Your double will do nothing for you except help declarer judge the bidding and then the play. They might be about to bid four hearts going down two. But after your helpful hint, they may stop in three hearts and then add insult to injury by making it.

DOUBLES OF FOURTH SUIT BIDS

Do not overlook this double. I often see opportunities like this overlooked at the table.

W	N	E	S
	1♢	Pass	1♡
Pass	1♠	Pass	2♣
Dbl			

♠J63 ♡10873 ♢4 ♣AQ987

South is using what they call a Fourth Suit bid. In today's bridge world, bidding the fourth suit to create a forcing auction is quite common. Give South a hand like this one.

♠K74 ♡AJ652 ♢AJ ♣1062

South responded one heart, which was easy, but when North rebid one spade, South was stuck. What bid should he make? He can't jump in spades, because opener is known to have only four. He can't emphasize hearts, because he has just five. Jumping in hearts would promise six. He can't bid notrump without a club stopper. He can't support diamonds, because he has just two of them.

The bid that is left is two clubs, a Fourth Suit bid. Most partnerships play that the fourth suit (defined here as the fourth suit at the two or three level) is forcing to game or very close to it. The problem that South has on this hand is often solved by bidding two clubs on what turns out to be a nonexistent holding. This is actually pretty logical because on some hands where South has a stopper in clubs, he can just bid notrump.

Hence West's double with the hand he has. If North is going to bid notrump, likely, West very much wants a club lead. Double is how to get it.

What if they redouble and make it?

If this happens, someone will get out a computer to sort out the score. When they figure it out, you will know instantly that you have a terrible board. It can happen. Good results are not risk-free, just like the stock market.

DOUBLES OF GERBER OR BLACKWOOD AUCTIONS

You can make lead directing doubles of Gerber or Blackwood responses to good effect. One thing you should be very sure of is that your partner is going to be on lead. If you double and end up on lead, you have gained nothing except to tell the opponents something about your hand.

Be sure also that if you get the lead you ask for it will work out for you. Bobby Goldman, one of the great players of our time and a good friend and partner of mine, once doubled a Blackwood answer of five spades with his K10643. The next player had been wondering whether to bid six or seven notrump. Holding the AQJ of spades, he knew this finesse was going to be onside and bid seven. Goldman was later seen shredding the king of spades.

DOUBLES OF DRURY

Do you play Drury? If not, I recommend it to you highly. It works this way. Your partner opens a major in third or fourth seat. If you have ten or more points and support, you show it by bidding two clubs. Two clubs is artificial, saying nothing about clubs. This is a fine convention which you are likely to encounter. If so, you have yet one more opportunity to double an artificial bid, and you should not miss the chance when holding an appropriate hand.

W	N	E	S
	Pass	Pass	1♡
Pass	2♣	Dbl	

There are two sensible ways to play a double of two clubs. It can be lead directing or for takeout.

You can use double to show good clubs. In this instance, your partner may have some values so your double should be two edged. It should show you want a club lead and it should imply enough values that you are willing for your partner to bid something.

♠K4 ♡87 ◇J842 ♣AQJ74

This hand would like a club lead, which double suggests. This hand, being a passed hand, is also pretty good. If your partner wishes to compete, usually in clubs, you do not mind.

♠8743 ♡43 ◇83 ♣KQ984

Not good enough to double. You want a club lead, but that is all. You do not want your partner to bid anything.

If you are willing to push the envelope, you can double with just clubs and otherwise poor hands. This gets your partner off to good leads, but it may cost you a number of hands where the hand actually belongs to your side. My preference is to have the double show clubs plus some values. Be my guest if you would like to experiment.

A lesser known treatment for a double of Drury two clubs is to play it for takeout.

W	N	E	S
			Pass
Pass	1♠	Pass	2♣
Dbl			

If you play that double is takeout, you can make a takeout double at this point and not wait until they finish their bidding.

♠62 ♡K743 ◇AJ8 ♣QJ106

Doubling two clubs with this hand does a couple of good things. It lets you double without risk. Your side can keep the bidding lower than if you pass and later decide to double two spades. If you wait and get a chance to double two spades, your partner has to bid at the three level. If you double two clubs, he can bid his suit at the two level or pass if his suit is clubs. Further, if he does bid at the three level, he will have something.

Another good thing your double of two clubs does is that it makes sure you get to compete. Once in awhile, the opponents get higher than two spades, and you are not able to get into the bidding. By using the double of two clubs as takeout, you ensure that you won't lose out if your partner has enough shape to make bidding worthwhile. This kind of thing can happen.

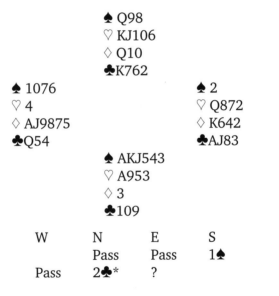

♠ Q98
♡ KJ106
◇ Q10
♣K762

♠ 1076
♡ 4
◇ AJ9875
♣Q54

♠ 2
♡ Q872
◇ K642
♣AJ83

♠ AKJ543
♡ A953
◇ 3
♣109

W	N	E	S
	Pass	Pass	1♠
Pass	2♣*	?	

Drury

If you pass, opener makes a game try or just bids a game directly. This will make if West leads a singleton heart or if South guesses hearts on his own. However, if you double two clubs for takeout, West will compete to five diamonds, thinking he is saving. Serendipity strikes — five diamonds makes with good guessing.

Both treatments have merit. Pick one.

DOUBLES OF SPLINTER BIDS

While splinter bids come in all shapes and forms, the basic splinter works like this.

W	N	E	S
1♡	Pass	4◇*	

Splinter

The double jump to a new suit shows a game forcing hand with a singleton in the suit bid. It allows opener to better evaluate his hand.

What does it mean if you double a splinter bid? There are two popular treatments in use and both of them are awful. Here are the two main choices in use today.

1.   It asks partner to lead the splinter suit.

2.   It tells your partner that you are willing to compete in the splinter suit if partner judges he has the right hand.

Say the bidding goes as shown above and you are thinking of doubling four diamonds.

1.   Example of a double if you wish a diamond lead:

♠J1093 ♡7 ◇KQ1065 ♣J52

You can double with this, but what have you really gained? Your partner will lead a diamond, which does nothing except perhaps stop him from leading something else to disadvantage. I can see using this double when you can't stand other leads. Keeping partner from making a bad lead is notable. If there is a better treatment for double, however, I would look for it.

2.   Example of a double if you wish to compete in diamonds:

♠96 ♡3 ◇AQ9865 ♣K952

You have a hand which suggests a five diamond sacrifice might work out. Your double encourages partner, with an appropriate hand, to bid five diamonds. Obviously, you cannot bid it yourself, especially when South has a singleton diamond. This warns you that any missing diamonds will be offside.

This might be a useful tactic, but I have not seen many cases where this double might be tried and even fewer cases where it would have worked. Here is my suggestion.

Play That a Double of a Splinter Bid Is Lead Directing but Not for the Splinter Suit

W	N	E	S
	1♡	Pass	4◇
?			

North bids one heart and South makes a splinter bid of four diamonds. Here are two possible hands for West to think about.

♠KQ109 ♡43 ◇J8763 ♣J3

♠J8763 ♡43 ◇J3 ♣KQ109

On the first hand you would love a spade lead. On the second hand you would be equally pleased with a club lead. What are the chances that your partner will find the right lead? If your partner has to guess, your chances of his finding the right lead are not that good. Here is my suggestion, which will greatly improve your partner's opening leads.

Double of a Splinter Bid Asks for the Lowest Unbid Suit. If you double four diamonds, you are telling your partner to lead the lowest unbid suit. On some auctions there is just one unbid suit. In this case your double tells partner to lead it. That suit might even be spades, but if spades is the only unbid suit, that is the one you want. If by some chance all four suits have been bid, the double calls for the lead of the lowest suit that is not trump.

Using this guideline on the two hands above, you would pass on the first hand and double on the second hand. This treatment always gets you a club lead on the second hand, and it gives your partner an inference on the first hand. Your partner will consider that if you do not double the splinter bid, you cannot want a club lead. He might just deduce that you want a spade lead. He can't be sure but he does have a valid inference.

Here are some example auctions with discussions.

W	N	E	S
	1♡	Pass	4♢
Dbl			

You want a club lead, the lowest unbid suit.

W	N	E	S
			1♢
Pass	1♡	Pass	4♣
Dbl			

South's four club bid was a splinter bid showing heart support. Your double asks for the lowest unbid suit, spades in this case.

W	N	E	S
	1♢	Pass	1♡
Pass	1♠	Pass	4♣
Dbl			

All three suits other than the splinter suit have been bid. Your double asks for a diamond lead. This seems odd since North bid the suit on your left. However, in the interests of not having a mix-up, it is wise to have a rule that you can stick to.

W	N	E	S
	2♣	Pass	2♢
Pass	2♡	Pass	4♢
Dbl			

On this auction, the only suit that has been 'bid' is hearts. Your double asks for a club lead.

This last idea is a mixed gift that I have toyed with for awhile. When the opponents splinter, you might wish to use a double as takeout of their major suit.

W	N	E	S
	1♡	Pass	4◇
Dbl			

♠Q983 ♡— ◇KJ83 ♣QJ872

You rate to have a hand like this one. The beauty of this double is that it is free. The opponents won't play in four diamonds. They will bid four hearts or even higher. Your double allows you to get into the bidding at little cost. Partner will bid with an appropriate hand, otherwise he passes and the auction continues.

GATES DOUBLE

You pass and later double a one notrump opening bid. Since you cannot have a penalty double, it can be used for something else. This thought of pristine clarity is sufficiently unknown that even though I knew of the understanding, I never knew it was known as the *Gates Double*. Here is an example of how it works.

Say you are using Hamilton (also known as Cappelletti) against an opening one notrump bid. This convention works thusly.

Double	= Penalty
2♣	= An unknown one-suited hand
2◇	= Both majors
2♡	= Hearts and a minor
2♠	= Spades and a minor
2NT	= Minors

Not a bad convention. Rather popular, in fact. The bidding starts this way. You are West.

W	N	E	S
Pass	Pass	Pass	1NT
?			

For the moment, let's not worry about your hand. Let's just say that it has some shape, and you are thinking of bidding something. You review the available bids and reflect that the first bid on the list is double. It is for penalty. I ask you. Having passed already, can you really have a good enough hand to double one notrump for penalty?

The Gates convention recognizes this fact and suggests you use a double as something besides penalty. Perhaps double should show a club suit. Perhaps double should show both minors. Perhaps double should show both majors but with longer spades, a traditionally awkward hand to show.

You get the idea. With no need for a penalty double, you can choose from a variety of good meanings for hands that otherwise might be unbiddable. All three of these ideas have merit, and unless you have a better one to offer, I would choose one of these. Perhaps using double to show the minors is best because it gives your partnership two choices of suits to compete in.

Give Gates a try. NOTE that the Gates double is used only as an adjunct to conventions that incorporate a penalty double of one notrump. If you are using a convention such as DONT, you do not make any changes in your system.

For the sake of explanation, here is what the DONT bids show over one notrump.

Double	= Single suited hand
2♣	= Clubs and another suit
2♢	= Diamonds and a Major
2♡	= Hearts and Spades
2♠	= Spades

You can show spades in two ways. You can bid two spades and you can double, showing a one-suited hand. If you bid two spades, you show a weaker hand than if you double and then show spades. As you can see, you need to use double as a one-suited hand in DONT regardless of whether you are a passed hand.

PHONY DOUBLE OF CUE BIDS

Care to try something that is guaranteed to confuse everyone at the table? Welcome to the Phony Double. It works like this.

```
                    ♠ 10873
                    ♡ A42
                    ◇ KQ632
                    ♣9
    ♠ 2                             ♠ J6
    ♡ KQJ9                          ♡ 10765
    ◇ 10954                         ◇ AJ7
    ♣6543                           ♣Q872
                    ♠ AKQ954
                    ♡ 83
                    ◇ 8
                    ♣AKJ10
```

W	N	E	S
			1♠
Pass	3♠	Pass	4♣
Dbl	Rdbl	Pass	4◇
Pass	4♡	Pass	4NT
Pass	5◇	Pass	6♠
Pass	Pass	Pass	

North and South arrived in six spades by South. It is cold with any lead except a heart, but that is the lead that South gets. Still, slam is a favorite. South wins the king of hearts lead and draws trump. His plan is to lead the ace and king of clubs and then the jack, picking up West's queen. Later he will discard dummy's heart and will concede a diamond for twelve tricks.

But there is bad news. Just because West doubled four clubs does not mean he has the queen. East has it and South goes down one. South could have made his slam by finessing East for the queen of clubs but that felt wrong after West's double.

Meet the Phony Double. West, a well known expert, has made quite a few of these doubles, and since they often lead to a swing for someone or another, they get publicity. Hence, those of us who read a lot know of this player's propensity to use the Phony Double. Those who do not follow the press are unaware of this habit.

This bidding trick can work. In fact, the better declarer is, the more likely he will go wrong in the play. Good players can be very creative when they have useful information from the bidding. The fact that the information they have is tainted is just unlucky.

Try this double if you wish. Oh, yes. If your partner starts using this double regularly, it becomes an alert. Since you will be aware that your partner is prone to using it, the opponents are entitled to know, also. So far, the well known expert's partner has not alerted this bid, or at least has not done so to my knowledge. That might be an error.

DOUBLES OF A STRONG ONE NOTRUMP BID, STAYMAN AND JACOBY

Penalty Double of a Strong Notrump

Many players today do not double strong notrump bids for penalty. They use a conventional double to show any of a number of possible hands. However, the penalty double is still popular, and if you use a double of one notrump for penalty, you need an agreement about what it shows.

To double a strong notrump (14-16 or more), whether in the immediate seat or in the reopening seat, you need a solid hand with a minimum of sixteen points. You can double with fifteen, if you have an excellent lead available. NOTE that in the reopening seat it is not all that safe to bid since you have no assurance that the dummy on your right does not have six or seven points.

Some players like to double one notrump in the pass out seat with ten or eleven points. I promise you this is a lousy idea. Even if you catch your partner with ten or more points, you will still have to defend well to take your tricks. I know of many doubled one notrump hands that could have been set but were allowed to escape, sometimes with overtricks.

Continuations after a Penalty Double, RHO Passes

One important theme in bidding when your partner doubles a strong notrump is that you tend to pass on all balanced hands. It is when you have shape that you tend to run and only then when your methods permit it. It is not terrible to use Stayman and Jacoby in response to partner's penalty double. Feel free to do so, but only with agreement. Two notrump should show the minors, although it is possible to play it shows a big two-suited hand that does not fall into your system otherwise.

♠4 ♡QJ974 ◇532 ♣9764

It is sensible to bid two hearts by whichever methods your partnership has chosen to use. If you use natural bidding, bid two hearts. Your partner won't play you for much. If you are using Jacoby and Stayman, bid two diamonds, asking partner to bid two hearts.

♠4 ♡532 ◇9764 ♣QJ974

If you do not have a way to get to two clubs with this hand, it is sensible to pass and hope for something good to happen.

Continuations after a Penalty Double, RHO Bids

W	N	E	S
1NT*	Dbl	2♡	?

strong

First, a double by you now should be used as takeout of the suit bid (spades in the auction above, if two hearts is a transfer) showing enough points that you wish your partner to bid. Plus, you can add some Lebensohl methods as well. Play that two notrump forces partner to bid three clubs. You will pass three clubs if you have a competitive hand with clubs and bid three diamonds with a competitive hand with diamonds. Bidding a suit at the three level is natural and forcing. You can come up with all kinds of tricks here if you like to experiment. At the very least, you should know what your bids mean.

Doubles of Jacoby Transfers

W	N	E	S
1NT	Pass	2♡*	?

Transfer

Doubling a Jacoby bid should just be lead directing. If you are playing matchpoints, feel free to use this double liberally. If your double gains you just one trick, that will usually be worth a good score. You will gain on more hands than not. Even if you suffer some real disasters, such as two hearts redoubled making, you will come out ahead. At IMPs you have to be more careful. You cannot afford to get bad results at IMPs the way you can afford to at matchpoints.

♠764 ♡KQ1085 ◇76 ♣A53

This is a great hand for doubling two hearts. A heart lead may establish your suit immediately and your club ace will be an entry. I would make this double at matchpoints or IMPs.

♠63 ♡KJ984 ◇432 ♣KJ8

This hand is weaker, yet it is reasonable to double at matchpoints. There is no reason why a heart lead should not be effective if your partner is on lead. At IMPs, this is scarier because it is possible that two hearts doubled could become the final contract. I think I would risk this at IMPs, but this is as weak as it gets.

♠J3 ♡KQJ9 ◇874 ♣9873

At matchpoints, go ahead and double. If your partner leads the two of hearts against three notrump, you feel great. If you pass and he leads the two of clubs or diamonds against three notrump, you feel that you would have preferred a different lead. The main thing to mention here is that you can do something to improve your partner's leads.

Doubles of Stayman

If your opponents are using a strong notrump, a double of two clubs, Stayman, should be lead directing. This is the same agreement that exists over a Jacoby transfer bid. You want to help partner find a good lead. The only question is how aggressive do you want to be with your doubles.

W	N	E	S
1NT	Pass	2♣	?

♠A63 ♡KQ74 ◇J73 ♣AJ3

Best is to pass and let partner choose a good opening lead. If you double, you will get a club lead, something you do not really want to insist on.

♠87 ♡A653 ◇53 ♣KJ1097

Try a double. If they get to any notrump contract, you know that your partner will lead one of your doubleton suits. If you double you will get a club lead and with luck, this will be enough to set the contract. At the least, you will usually gain a trick as opposed to what partner's choice of leads will get you.

♠763 ♡3 ◇J8653 ♣AKJ10

Double with this, too. At IMPs it is easy to make a case for passing, but the benefit of getting a club lead is so tempting that many players would take the risk of doubling.

DOUBLES OF A WEAK ONE NOTRUMP BID, STAYMAN AND JACOBY

This is an area of bidding that has not had much written about it and I do not have so much experience that I am confident about what one should do. This section covers a variety of situations that occur when the opponents start with a weak notrump. Do not look at this chapter as having answers. Look at it as offering questions and a few suggestions.

Penalty Double of a Weak Notrump

Almost all players use a double of a weak notrump for penalty. If you use a double this way, you need some agreements to make it work. If you double a weak notrump (13-15 or less) for penalty, you need a good fourteen or more points if your hand is balanced. Even if their range is as low as ten to twelve, it is wise to have a fourteen count or better for a penalty double.

♠QJ74 ♡KJ3 ◇QJ4 ♣A84

I would not double with this against any size notrump. You have fourteen points but no clear lead. Best to let this kind of hand go quietly.

♠A3 ♡QJ1074 ◇AQ8 ♣J63

A fourteen count which has a good lead. This is about as weak as I would have for a double of one notrump, even of the ten to twelve variety. NOTE that bidding two hearts is not a good idea. You have a balanced hand which suggests defending.

You can also double with some shapely hands if you have long suits you expect to run.

119

♠A ♡K64 ♢KQJ964 ♣Q74

Doubling with this is OK too. Your partner will not expect this hand, however. He will assume you have a balanced hand.

RULE—*Do Not Bid with Weak Hands Against a Weak Notrump*

If you bid a suit against a weak notrump, or if you use a convention against a weak notrump, you should have a decent hand. It is not wise to fight against a weak notrump with weak hands. The reason is that your partner will think that there could be a game contract, and he will look for one if he has a fair hand. It is fine to bid against a STRONG notrump with weak hands, because you hope to distract their bidding. It is unlikely that you have a game when they open a strong notrump, so your partner will know not to take you seriously.

Here is a scheme of bids that your partnership can use over a weak notrump. One of them is going to be a big surprise.

Dbl   As I discussed above, this bid shows a balanced hand in the fourteen to seventeen point range. You might even have a good eighteen to twenty points. If you have this fine a hand and your partner bids something, you usually find a second bid to let partner know that you have more than he expects. Double also includes other types of good hands that do not have an easy immediate bid. If your hand is too good to overcall or to use an artificial bid such as DONT or Cappelletti, you might start with a double.

2♣   Two clubs and all other suit bids can be used to show whatever your convention of choice calls for.

2NT   Surprise. This should be used to show a strong two notrump bid. It is NOT unusual for the minors. The range is twenty-one to twenty-two, although you can use judgment with twenty point and twenty-three point hands. This may seem like a silly way to bid over their weak notrump but since you can also double with fifteen or so, your partner is going to have difficulties knowing what to do after your double.

Bidding After Partner Doubles a Weak Notrump

RULE—*In general, with a few points or with a balanced hand, you tend to pass the double. When you bid, you usually have a weak hand and your partner should assume this unless you later show you have real points.*

RHO Passes

W	N	E	S
	1NT	Dbl	Pass
?			

A useful tactic exists when your partner doubles one notrump. Since his double usually shows a balanced hand with a minimum range of points, you can use Stayman and Jacoby just as if your partner had opened one notrump.

W	N	E	S
	1NT	Dbl	Pass
2♣			

Asks for a major. This does not promise anything. All you are trying to do is reach a sensible contract of your own.

W	N	E	S
	1NT	Dbl	Pass
2♢			

A transfer to hearts. You usually have a poor hand but you might have a hand that wants to show hearts first and then bid again.

W	N	E	S
	1NT	Dbl	Pass
2♠			

How do you currently use a two spade response to one notrump? Is it a transfer to clubs? Does it show both minors? You can continue to use the two spade bid as you normally do, but be aware that it shows a weak hand instead of a good one.

W	N	E	S
	1NT	Dbl	Pass
2NT			

How about a two notrump response? Perhaps this should be a transfer to clubs. If you do this, you might play three clubs is a transfer to diamonds.

Remember— If you use one of these tricks, you rate to have a weak hand. With a good hand you would just pass, trying to collect a juicy penalty. Partner needs to be on the same wavelength.

1.   When you respond with Stayman or Jacoby to your partner's double, he must remember that you are likely to have a weak hand. Only rarely will he do anything other than to make his normal response.

2.   On rare occasions the doubler will have a huge hand. If he doubles and gets a Stayman or Jacoby bid from his partner, he must not make a simple response, since it is likely that this will end the bidding. One way to handle this is for the doubler to bid two notrump in response to the Stayman or Jacoby bid to announce he has at least a super eighteen points up to a fair twenty. When this happens, responder starts all over by bidding his Stayman or Jacoby bid but this time at the three level. A second way to show one of these good hands is to jump in a suit that your partner is showing. See an example of this below.

3.   There is a downside to these treatments in that you cannot play two clubs, and only occasionally can you play two diamonds. You have to judge if this is too big a price to pay.

W	N	E	S
			1NT
Dbl	Pass	2♣	Pass
2♠	Pass	Pass	Pass

♠ KJ64	♠ 10983
♡ 107	♡ Q8632
◇ AKQ8	◇ 2
♣K103	♣986

West doubles with his sixteen high card points but finds East with a lousy hand. East scrambles out of one notrump, doubled, with two clubs, asking for a major. East's intention is to pass if West bids a major and to bid two hearts, showing both majors, if partner bids two diamonds. On this hand West has spades so a fit is found. Would that you were always so lucky in this situation.

W	N	E	S
			1NT
Dbl	Pass	2♡	Pass
2NT	Pass	3♡	Pass
3♠	Pass	Pass	Pass

♠ AK	♠ J10853
♡ KQ9	♡ J10
◇ QJ7	◇ 10984
♣A8743	♣92

East runs from one notrump, doubled, this time by using Jacoby. West does not want to bid two spades because he has a mountain. He shows this by bidding two notrump, which shows about eighteen to twenty points. East then starts all over and West plays in a nervous three spades.

♠ 6	♠ J10853
♡ KQ6	♡ J10
◇ AK5	◇ 10984
♣AQ10764	♣92

West cannot accept the transfer with this hand either. He bids three clubs, showing that he does not like spades but has a good club suit.

W	N	E	S
			1NT
Dbl	Pass	2♣	Pass
3♠	Pass	Pass	Pass

♠ KQ976	♠ J542
♡ KQ	♡ 9874
◇ K74	◇ Q985
♣AQ10	♣4

West does not want to bid two spades here. With five of them, it is OK to jump to three spades, suggesting that he has a hand worth more than the expected fifteen to seventeen. This jump suggests a hand in the eighteen to twenty point range. East has to judge his hand in light of this new information and probably chooses to pass three spades. NOTE that East is obviously prepared to hear West bid two spades so East should not be embarrassed to hear three spades from West. This treatment might get you too high but if responder has six or seven support points for spades, you may reach a good game. If West had one less spade, he should bid two notrump over two clubs. East would continue by bidding three clubs, intending to pass whatever West bid.

One small, unrelated point is that when you play the hand, you will know where the high card points are so your guesses ought to be successful more often than not.

RHO Bids

W	N	E	S
	1NT	Dbl	2♣
?			

For once, life is easy. Play that doubling two clubs shows a Stayman hand and two diamonds or hearts are transfer bids. This theme comes up in a number of ways in this general area of bidding.

W	N	E	S
	1NT	Dbl	2◊
?			

If two diamonds is natural, double is Stayman, not Stolen Bid. Two hearts and spades are natural and since you did not have to bid, you promise a few points. If you like, you can use Lebensohl methods as well over two diamonds.

If two diamonds is a transfer to hearts, you have lots of choices. One that is easy enough is to say that when you double a transfer bid, you are making a takeout double of the major that they are showing. Here, if you double two diamonds, your meaning is takeout of hearts. If you bid two hearts, this can be used to show competitive values in the minor suits.

♠KJ43 ♡83 ◊Q983 ♣Q94

Double to show a takeout double of hearts. You happen to have four diamonds too. That is an accident. You might have only three of them.

♠873 ♡5 ◊QJ87 ♣KJ983

Bid two hearts. This says you are willing to compete in a minor suit. With a better hand you will bid again after partner shows his best minor. Keep in mind that he does not have to bid a minor. He can bid spades or notrump too if he wishes.

Two notrump ought to be Lebensohl, telling your partner to bid three clubs.

W	N	E	S
	1NT	Dbl	2♡
?			

Here is a list of the tools you have to choose from.

Dbl   If two hearts is natural, this is a takeout double of hearts; if two hearts is a transfer to spades, this is a takeout double of spades. You show seven or more points with takeout shape. You could have other hands but this is the one your partner will expect. Note that this double is not for penalty, it is value-showing and suggests but does not guarantee the other major. If you wish to double two hearts for penalty, you must pass, hoping that your partner can double for takeout.

♠873 ♡KJ873 ◇108 ♣Q74

You must pass with this hand. If you double, your partner will take it out, thinking it is a takeout double.

RULE—*If your side doubles a weak notrump, your side's next double is takeout. Once your side makes a takeout double, all subsequent doubles are for penalty.*

2♠ Assuming two hearts is natural, two spades is competitive, showing five spades and seven or so points. If two hearts showed spades, a two spade bid can be used to show a competitive hand with the minors.

2NT You can use Lebensohl here fairly successfully. Two notrump tells partner to bid three clubs. You may have clubs but you may also have another suit to show. Your next bid will clarify. In any case, if you bid two notrump, you promise a few values.

RULE—*If you wish to bid a suit that is higher ranking than the one bid on your right, you have three ways to do it.*

1.   With a modest hand, bid two of the suit.
2.   Jump in the suit. This is forcing.
3.   Use Lebensohl and then bid the suit. This is invitational.

RULE—*If you wish to bid a suit that is lower ranking than the one bid on your right, you have two ways to do it.*

1.   Bid the suit directly at the three level. This is forcing.
2.   Use Lebensohl and then bid the suit. This is invitational.

RULE—*Doubles are takeout of whichever suit your RHO is showing.*

RULE—*If your RHO uses a transfer bid, a cue bid shows the minor suits with invitational or greater values.*

RHO Redoubles

W	N	E	S
	1NT	Dbl	Rdbl
?			

If the redouble is for penalty, you may well wish to escape. Stayman and transfers do not work well because you cannot get to two of a minor. I suggest that if you have a balanced hand, you pass and let partner choose the method of escape. If you bid a suit it is natural and passable, including two clubs and two diamonds. If you bid something and it gets doubled as you expect, a redouble is for takeout, saying that you want partner to choose from the higher ranking suits.

♠10874 ♡9873 ♢8732 ♣2

You can try two clubs, not because it is asking for another suit but because it avoids having to defend against one notrump, redoubled. You expect someone to double two clubs and you will redouble to tell your partner to choose another suit. If two clubs is passed out (virtually impossible) you go down five or six, but at least it is an undoubled five or six. Also, you have a story. If you redouble and your partner fails to take it out, you won't have to tell your friends about it. Your opponents will do that for you.

♠865432 ♡3 ♢876 ♣652

Two spades. If you are so lucky as to have a six card suit, bid it.

♠62 ♡976 ♢J932 ♣8762

Treat this as balanced and pass. Your partner will know by now that he probably chose a bad moment for the double and hopefully he has a spot that he can escape to.

W	N	E	S
	1NT	Dbl	Pass*

*Forces redouble

Sometimes you will run into this convention. South's pass tells opener to redouble. South may have a good hand, but he may also have a hand that wants to escape from one notrump. His pass is part of his escape method. Should you encounter this convention, you may wish to do this.

Bidding a suit immediately shows a one-suited hand, usually a weak one. Passing and then bidding after the redouble shows a two-suited hand, the suit bid and a higher ranking one.

W	N	E	S
	1NT	Dbl	Pass*
Pass	Rdbl	Pass	Pass
?			

Forces redouble

South's auction says he thinks his partner can make one notrump, redoubled.

♠10874 ♡J7653 ◇43 ♣53

If I had this hand I would agree with South's opinion. The way to escape is to pass on the first round, allowing opener to redouble, and when that gets back, bid two hearts. Your two heart bid says you have hearts and a higher suit, which must be spades. Your partner will choose a major, after which the real fun begins.

If your RHO bids after the redouble, showing a weak hand of some sort, double by you is for takeout. You must also play that a pass by you forces partner to keep the auction alive below two spades.

W	N	E	S
	1NT	Dbl	Pass*
Pass	Rdbl	Pass	2◇
?			

*Forces Redouble

♠Q983 ♡AJ84 ◇873 ♣84

It looks like South may have wiggled out. You should double with this hand, which is basically takeout, trying to let partner know you do have something. South, remember, may have a pretty poor hand if he is running from one notrump. The hand probably belongs to your side in spite of their trumpeting noises in the auction.

If you wish to double them, you must pass and hope that partner can double.

♠984 ♡J5 ◇AQ987 ♣873

After your forcing pass, your partner will have to bid. He may be able to make a takeout double, which you will pass. In addition to using doubles as takeout and a pass as forcing against two hearts or lower, you can also play some Lebensohl sequences too. Eric Kokish would be proud of any pair that understands these sequences perfectly. I can tell you that I do not yet qualify for his kind words in this area. Perhaps when he writes a book.

Partner Passes, RHO Bids Stayman or Jacoby

Bidding over Stayman and Jacoby is easy enough after they open a strong notrump but after a weak notrump opening bid, life is not so easy.

W	N	E	S
	1NT	Pass	2♣
?			

W	N	E	S
	1NT	Pass	2◇
?			

When they are using a weak notrump, your side will often have the majority of the points. West may have a pretty good hand when the bidding starts this way. The modern treatment is to play a double of either Stayman or Jacoby is value showing, not lead directing. You should double with most balanced hands containing at least fourteen high card points up to much better hands that do not have a clear bid to make. These hands would all double a Stayman or a Jacoby transfer over a weak notrump opener.

♠AK8 ♡873 ◇K102 ♣A983

♠AQJ ♡K2 ◇642 ♣AKQ86

♠K74 ♡A74 ◇AKJ83 ♣Q7

The double does not emphasize the suit bid, although you may have a strong holding in it. The reason this treatment is useful is that it allows your side to get into the bidding when you have a good hand. Remember that weak notrumpers are on this earth to steal from you. If you allow them to do this, you will suffer for it. A plague on weak notrump bidders.

W	N	E	S
	1NT	Pass	2♣
?			

W	N	E	S
	1NT	Pass	2◇
?			

♠QJ10743 ♡5 ◇KJ108 ♣54

Pass. If you bid two spades, your partner will often have enough points to raise, which you do not want. Better to pass now and bid two spades later if you can. Remember, it is not wise to bid with a weak hand against the weak notrump.

♠AKJ984 ♡43 ◇85 ♣KJ9

Bid two spades against a weak notrump for sure. Your side may own the hand and if so, you need to be in the bidding. The rule is that against weak notrump bidders an overcall shows nice, not competitive values. (Against a strong notrump you can bid two spades, but it is not as safe since your LHO has around sixteen points, not thirteen.)

♠AKJ4 ♡Q94 ◇AQ8 ♣KJ3

Two Notrump! This is odd, since you normally use two notrump to show the minors. Against weak notrump bidders, they are likely to be stealing and you need a way to show good hands like this one. If you do not wish to bid two notrump, at least double two clubs or two diamonds, not for the lead, but to show a generally good hand.

If they use a weak notrump and your partner doubles a Stayman or Jacoby response, your world becomes very complex. Your partner is not promising strength in the suit he is doubling, so you can't just pass and collect a penalty.

Here are a few of the issues you have to address:

> How do you bid when you have a lousy hand?
> How do you bid when you have an invitational hand?
> How do you bid when you have a good hand?
> How do you bid when opener passes after the double?
> How do you bid when opener bids after the double?

I started to write up a complete method and discovered that it would take nearly fifty pages, more than most players would want to read and more than this book has room for. I can give you a few ideas and leave the rest to enterprising partnerships to sort out.

W	N	E	S
			1NT
Pass	2◇	Dbl	Pass
?			

Pass   Since your partner does not promise he has values in the suit he doubled, you should not leave the double in unless you have four cards or more in the suit. A pass neither promises nor denies values.

2♡   One possibility is to play that bidding two of the major that the Jacoby bidder is looking for shows eight or more points and asks partner to bid a suit. You imply four cards in the unbid major.

2♠   Typically this shows five spades; you may bid a four card spade suit, although that is rare. You do deny values, though. If you have a good hand with eight or more points you should look for a stronger bid.

You can use Lebensohl treatments here too. Or, if you prefer, you can use three level transfer bids as well. If you do, you need to decide on all kinds of questions such as what a transfer into their major suit means.

W	N	E	S
			1NT
Pass	2♣	Dbl	Pass
?			

Pass   Your partner may have only two little clubs, perhaps even one, and that means you should not pass the double unless you have something good in clubs yourself. Usually this means four of them.

Lebensohl treatments work here, also. Two of a suit is non-forcing and could be a four card suit. Suit bids at the three level are forcing and two notrump followed by a new suit is invitational. Keep in mind that there is no cue bid available in this auction.

W	N	E	S
	1NT	Pass	2♣
Dbl	2◇	?	

W	N	E	S
	1NT	Pass	2◇
Dbl	2♡	?	

Once again, it is best to play that a double of opener's bid is takeout, not penalty. Using this treatment, you must have the agreement that if you pass and your partner doubles again, it is also for takeout. This means that neither you nor your partner can double opener's bid for penalty. Both of you can double for takeout, though. If this happens, you or your partner can pass with strength in their suit. In the event that your side does make a takeout double, all subsequent doubles are for business. On those occasions where opener does bid a suit, you can use a combination of natural bids and Lebensohl bids along the lines of when you open one notrump and they overcall. Here are a couple of example auctions.

♠ Q743	♠ A9
♡ 87	♡ A62
◇ K32	◇ Q10874
♣K1063	♣AJ4

W	N	E	S
			1NT
Pass	2◇	Dbl	2♡
Dbl	Pass	3◇	Pass
Pass	Pass		

West doubles two hearts and East takes it out to three diamonds. A sane contract is reached. It would be dangerous for East to compete to three diamonds unless West promised some values.

♠ 43		♠ AJ52	
♡ QJ962		♡ 5	
♢ A2		♢ KQ84	
♣ 8763		♣ AQ52	

W	N	E	S
			1NT
Pass	2♢	Dbl	2♡
Pass	Pass	Dbl	Pass
Pass	Pass		

West can't double two hearts, because that would be for takeout. He has to pass and hope that East can bid again. NOTE that East has a shapely hand. His double does not promise a balanced hand.

♠ Q832		♠ AJ	
♡ 62		♡ AJ87	
♢ A8		♢ Q1054	
♣ Q10963		♣ K52	

W	N	E	S
			1NT
Pass	2♣	Dbl	2♢
Dbl	2♡	Dbl	Pass
Pass	Pass		

East doubles two clubs to show general values. West doubles two diamonds for takeout. West's plan is to follow with two spades if East bids two hearts (with the same values and five spades, West would bid two spades instead of doubling). East doubles two hearts for penalty. Once your side makes a takeout double, all later doubles are for penalty.

RHO Opens a Weak Notrump, Partner Reopens with a Double

Not much to say here. Your partner's double requires the same values as an immediate double. You can choose to play Stayman and Jacoby if you like. A good point to talk to your partner about in advance.

If you like these ideas relating to competing against the weak notrump and the responses, I instruct you to root for Eric Kokish to put his other works aside for a few months and to do something he has been promising me for years. I can hear him speaking now, "I want to write a book on competitive bidding. I just don't have time right now." If you ever run into him, tell him to find some time. I apologize for giving such a brief discussion on this treatment. Hopefully, it will give you something to think about.

Doubles with a Penalty Overtone

There are a number of doubles related to penalties. Some of them are just plain 'gotcha' doubles where your opponents get into obvious trouble. Others include some lead directing qualities. Most players know of the Lightner Slam Double. Far fewer know that you can use this double to combat games and even partscores. Then there are a couple of doubles that seem to fit in here better than in any other section.

Fishbein Double

This double is very straightforward. An opponent opens with a preempt, and you double it for penalty. I suspect the world has given up on this and other conventions focusing on penalizing a preempt. I am mentioning it here only to shoot it down in case anyone is still using it.

It does not work. If you play Fishbein, you have to make a different bid when you want your partner to bid and that bid becomes overworked. If, for instance, they open three hearts and you use double for penalty, what do you bid when you want your partner to bid?

Do you bid three spades? If so, how do you show a hand with real spades? Do you use four clubs? If so, how do you show a hand with real clubs? And also, how can you stop in three spades when your partner has a lousy hand?

I suggest you play takeout doubles all the way through four spades. If you play penalty doubles of four spades, what do you do with the following hands?

♠2 ♡AQ73 ◇KQJ3 ♣AQ74

♠4 ♡6 ◇AQJ84 ♣AKJ964

♠— ♡QJ1087 ◇AKJ873 ♣KJ

The only bid you have to force your partner to bid is four notrump, the classic solution. The trouble is that you do not always have the first hand. Sometimes you have the second or the third hand. How can your poor partner know what to do when you bid four notrump if you can have all three of these hands? The answer is to play that double is takeout, showing the first hand, and four notrump shows two suits as in the second or third hand.

LIGHTNER SLAM DOUBLE

Most players have heard of the Lightner Slam Double. This is one of the most valuable doubles a defender has. The way they work is simple enough. When the opponents finish bidding to a slam, the player who is not on lead can double to instruct his partner what to lead. Normally the double says that he wants the lead of dummy's first bid suit, but there are sequences where the double just alerts the opening leader that something unusual is required. When this happens, the opening leader is supposed to look at his hand and sort out what is wanted. Here are examples of each.

$\spadesuit$ KJ986
$\heartsuit$ AQ84
$\diamondsuit$ KJ3
$\clubsuit$3

$\spadesuit$ 75432		$\spadesuit$ AQ
$\heartsuit$ 107		$\heartsuit$ 9653
$\diamondsuit$ 10986		$\diamondsuit$ 7542
$\clubsuit$J5		$\clubsuit$1062

$\spadesuit$ 10
$\heartsuit$ KJ2
$\diamondsuit$ AQ
$\clubsuit$AKQ9874

W	N	E	S
	1$\spadesuit$	Pass	2$\clubsuit$
Pass	2$\heartsuit$	Pass	4NT
Pass	5$\diamondsuit$	Pass	6NT
Pass	Pass	Dbl	Pass
Pass	Pass		

Look at East's hand. He expects that dummy will have the king of spades and if so, a spade lead will set six notrump immediately. His double asks West to make an unusual lead and in keeping with the general guideline, that lead should be a spade, dummy's first bid suit. With any other lead, South has all the tricks.

W	N	E	S
			3$\spadesuit$
Pass	4NT	Pass	5$\diamondsuit$
Pass	6$\spadesuit$	Dbl	Pass
Pass	Pass		

$\spadesuit$8 $\heartsuit$Q1095432 $\diamondsuit$QJ10 $\clubsuit$54

What should West lead?

Assuming no one is nuts, East is not doubling with two aces. That is a great way to get bad results. His double should be lead directing. The problem here is that the normal rule does not apply. Dummy never bid a suit other than spades, so you can't refer to the bidding to find out what East wants.

There is, however, a second part to the Lightner Double. It says that if the bidding does not give you a clue about what to lead, you should look at your hand to see if there is any hint there. Often your partner wants to ruff something, and he is telling you to look at your hand to see which suit he is ruffing.

On this hand you have seven hearts and that is a pretty good clue. If you lead a heart, they go down a trick. If you lead anything else, they make. Here is the complete hand.

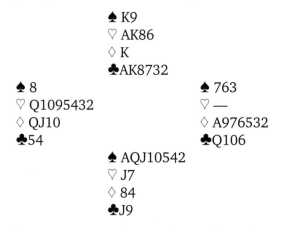

Poor South. He got to a great slam and went down because of a seven-zero heart split. The chances of that happening are around half of one percent. Nasty stuff.

LIGHTNER GAME DOUBLE

They Bid Three Notrump

Most of your Lightner type doubles will be against slams. Be aware that they work just as well against games, too. I estimate that about ninety percent of your lead directing game doubles will be against three notrump, but they can occur against suit contracts too. Here are a few situations where you might double three notrump. You are sitting East.

W	N	E	S
			1NT
Pass	3NT	?	

♠AKQJ74 ♡74 ◇84 ♣J42

Double. There are many variations on this double. The one I recommend is the *You-Figure-Out-What-Suit-I-Want* Double. If they bid three notrump as on this sequence, a double by you tells your partner to guess which suit you want and to lead it. Since your double will usually be on a long suit, your partner will tend to lead his short suit.

There is a double called the Fisher Double that asks for a club lead if no suits were bid and a diamond lead if Stayman was used but not doubled. There is another double (called, I believe, the Elwell Double) that asks for a heart lead. These doubles are narrow, focusing usually on one suit. The double I suggest here focuses on all suits and invites your partner's judgment.

W	N	E	S
			1NT
Pass	3NT	?	

♠75 ♡KQJ106 ◇A7 ♣9763

Double again and hope that partner finds a heart lead. If he does, you are a favorite to set three notrump. NOTE that if you do not double, you may be treated to partner's lead of the jack of diamonds, which will both remove your entry and set up a trick or two for declarer at the same time.

If the opponents get to three notrump after having bid some suits along the way, double tends to ask for dummy's first bid suit.

W	N	E	S
			1♣
Pass	1♡	Pass	1NT
Pass	3NT	?	

You should double three notrump with all of these hands.

♠873 ♡AKJ106 ◇1074 ♣82

♠84 ♡KQJ94 ◇643 ♣A83

♠A763 ♡QJ1084 ◇A2 ♣76

These doubles rate to get your side off to the best defense and often will be enough to set three notrump. While the opponents may make a few of these, one thing is clear. If your partner does not lead a heart, you have very little chance of success.

W	N	E	S
			1◇
1♡	2◇	2♡	2NT
Pass	3NT	?	

If you double, you are asking your partner to lead hearts. This would tend to be true even if you did not raise them.

W	N	E	S
			1◇
1♡	Dbl	2♣	2NT
Pass	3NT	?	

Here, both of you have bid a suit. It is possible to make a case for either lead. I have not seen enough of these auctions come up that I can claim a trend, but my inclination is that you want partner's suit led. My main recommendation here is that you agree, and then when this happens, you will always do the right thing.

W	N	E	S
			1◇
Pass	1♡	1♠	2◇
Pass	3◇	Pass	3NT
Pass	Pass	Dbl	Pass
Pass	Pass		

When you have done the only bidding for your side, a double demands that your partner lead your suit. You do not want your partner to get some bright idea that leading a club might be good. These, then, are the general rules surrounding doubles of three notrump.

1. If nobody bid a suit, your partner has to decide by looking at his hand which suit you want.

2. If dummy has bid a suit, your double usually asks for the lead of dummy's first suit.

3. If your side has bid just one suit, a double asks for that lead.

4. If your side has bid two suits, the double asks the opening leader to lead his suit.

They Bid Game in a Suit

Assuming the bidding has not been competitive and your double is unexpected, it rates to be lead directing. The double alerts your partner that something special is needed. He will try to sort it out.

W	N	E	S
			1♡
Pass	2◇	Pass	2♡
Pass	4♡	Dbl	Pass
Pass	Pass		

♠A74 ♡84 ◇J7654 ♣Q53

The opponents have just had a strong auction to reach four hearts. Do you think that your partner can have four or five top tricks in his own hand, assuming the opponents have a glimmer of what they are doing? Unlikely. Since you have the ace of spades, it is almost impossible for your partner to have four certain high card tricks. Given that you have two little hearts, it is almost impossible that your partner has four trump tricks. What does your partner have?

Once you recognize this situation, you will know what to think about. Your partner is not doubling with high cards. He is doubling because he has a void and wants to alert you to that. Here is the hand as it occurred.

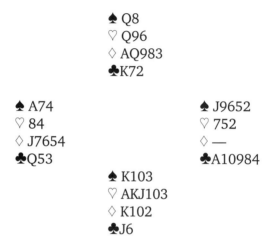

♠ Q8
♡ Q96
◇ AQ983
♣K72

♠ A74   ♠ J9652
♡ 84   ♡ 752
◇ J7654   ◇ —
♣Q53   ♣A10984

♠ K103
♡ AKJ103
◇ K102
♣J6

If West comes to the right conclusion, he will lead the seven of diamonds. East will ruff and return a spade. Another ruff and the ace of clubs will put four hearts down a trick. No other lead suffices.

There is a reason, by the way, for leading the seven of diamonds. West knows that East is ruffing diamonds and chooses the seven as a suit preference signal. Actually, West might even lead the jack, which would be even more emphatic.

W	N	E	S
		Pass	1♠
Pass	3♠	Pass	4♠
Pass	Pass	Dbl	Pass
Pass	Pass		

This is just another example of the same theme. East could not open the bidding, could not bid over three spades, and suddenly thinks he can set four spades. Not possible. Unless East has something special, which can only be a void.

RULE—*When the auction tells you it is impossible for partner to make a penalty double of a game contract and he does so, he is telling you he wants a special lead.*

Unlike the double of three notrump, the bidding often does not tell you what to lead. Instead, you must look at your hand to figure it out.

LIGHTNER PARTSCORE DOUBLE

Lead directing doubles of partscores? Yes. Believe it or not, the Lightner Double principles can be used against partscores too. This is a well kept secret that experts use to big advantage.

Almost always, lead directing doubles against partscores come against one or two notrump. These doubles occur when the opponents have shown limited values, and you know that their finesses are going to lose. Here are some examples.

W	N	E	S
			1◇
Pass	1♡	Pass	1NT
Pass	Pass	?	

Almost every lead directing double of one notrump occurs in balancing situations. If East were to double, what do you think it should mean? The majority of the world says it is a takeout double, but they are wrong. It should be a penalty double. Here is why.

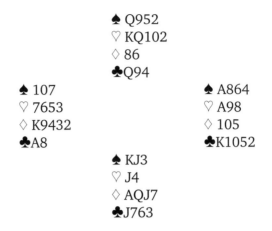

```
                    ♠ Q952
                    ♡ KQ102
                    ◇ 86
                    ♣Q94
    ♠ 107                          ♠ A864
    ♡ 7653                         ♡ A98
    ◇ K9432                        ◇ 105
    ♣A8                            ♣K1052
                    ♠ KJ3
                    ♡ J4
                    ◇ AQJ7
                    ♣J763
```

North and South bid diamonds and hearts and stopped in one notrump. The East hand has support for the unbid suits and that would cause many to double. Look what West has! West can't support either of East's suits. He has only two spades and only two clubs. How would you feel if you held the West hand and your partner asked you to choose between spades and clubs? Pretty disgusting.

The key is that North and South could not find a fit, which suggests that your side does not have a fit either. Even though they bid hearts and diamonds, they have more cards in the unbid suits, spades and clubs. Happens.

The correct usage for double when the opponents bid back and forth to one notrump is penalty.

W	N	E	S
			1♡
Pass	1♠	Pass	1NT
Pass	Pass	?	

♠KJ1076 ♡2 ◇A763 ♣KQ8

You know that their side has around half of the points on average. They may have a few more, but they may have less. You also know that any finesses they take in hearts will lose because your partner is sitting with heart length over declarer's heart length. And, you have fine spades that you wish partner to lead. If you double and if your partner understands what you mean, he will lead a spade. Here is the complete hand.

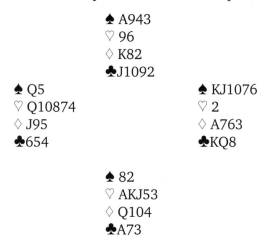

There is some good news and some bad news. The bad news is that South has a nice maximum, and North has a solid eight count. The good news is that West has the queen of spades and knows enough to lead it. The result of this lead is devastating to South. If he gives the hand best play, he can go down one but if he decides to play on hearts, he rates to do down a couple. Compare what happens if East does not double. West may not find a spade lead, and his other choice, whatever it is, will not be good for the defense.

You may think that this double does not come up often enough to be worthwhile. Just yesterday while playing on one of the online bridge clubs, this hand occurred. I sat West with both sides vulnerable. The opponents had a routine auction to one notrump. What should happen next?

```
                       ♠ 943
                       ♡ AQ752
                       ◇ Q876
                       ♣2
        ♠ AJ8                           ♠ Q76
        ♡ 964                           ♡ KJ8
        ◇ K4                            ◇ 10932
        ♣KQJ94                          ♣863
                       ♠ K1052
                       ♡ 103
                       ◇ AJ5
                       ♣A1075
```

W	N	E	S
			1♣
Pass	1♡	Pass	1♠
Pass	1NT	Pass	Pass
?			

When you play online, you often play with someone who is not on your wavelength. On this hand, I decided to risk a double of one notrump, and if it had played there, a club lead would have set it a lot. You can figure out the damages yourself. We never did find out how many one notrump would go down, because East thought the double was takeout and bid two diamonds. Whatever you think of that bid, it is clear that our side lost a nice opportunity.

Doubling two notrump for penalty is a profitable action if you go about it properly. Mind you, the right times are specific, and the circumstances must be right for this double to be proper. If you get it right, though, you will do very, very well. Here are some guidelines.

1.   The opponents have stopped in two notrump.
2.   You want partner to lead dummy's first suit.

Here are some example auctions. You are East.

W	N	E	S
			1♢
Pass	1♠	Pass	2♣
Pass	2♢	Pass	2NT
Pass	Pass	?	

This is an auction that does not have to be successful. South typically has about seventeen points (that is what he should have), but if North is really weak and if the hands do not fit well, eight tricks may be hard to get.

♠AQ108 ♡32 ◇J1063 ♣653

Doubling two notrump is quite reasonable. You know that they have limited values and you know you have spades stopped plus your spade spots give you the potential to take four tricks. Those spade spots are very important. If your spades were AQ32, you would not double. Also, you have a diamond stopper.

There is more good news. Since they have around twenty-two or twenty-three points, you can infer that your partner will have ten or eleven himself. Your double is not just you alone. Your partner definitely will contribute something. Finally, you must consider your partner's opening lead. He is likely to lead hearts and you hate that. If he leads from the Q10865 of hearts, it will do your side no good. It costs a trick right away, and it gives the lead to their side. Much better if your partner leads a spade. If things work well for you, you could set this two or three tricks.

How often will your double work? That is something that I would have to guess at. My feeling is that on this sequence, assuming your opponents are competent bidders, you will set them frequently without your doubling them. However, by doubling them, I estimate you will set them around seventy-five percent of the time or more. Oddly, you have a better chance of success with this double against sound opposition than against bad opposition. Good opponents bid aggressively and accurately. Weak opponents are capable of getting to two notrump with twenty-five points, which would make it hard to beat.

W	N	E	S
			Pass
Pass	1♡	Pass	2NT
Pass	Pass	?	

♠73 ♡KJ107 ◇AJ74 ♣A93

Double. On this auction you have an extra reason to be optimistic. North may have been frisky with his opening bid. If he opened with a ten or eleven point hand and South is jumping to two notrump with eleven points, you may kill them. They will need good luck to make eight tricks with twenty-one points, and you know they aren't getting any.

Basically, most close contracts depend on a modicum of luck. If you are a defender and you can see that declarer is going to be unlucky, feel free to double two notrump and let declarer pay for his bad luck. NOTE this big distinction between doubling two notrump and doubling three notrump. When your opponents stop in two notrump, you know almost exactly how many high card points they hold. They rate to have around twenty-two or twenty-three. With more than that, they bid game.

When they go on to three notrump, you have to worry that they may have three or four extra points. It is possible. So when you are thinking of doubling three notrump, you need to consult the bidding to make sure they do not have enough extra points to overcome the bad luck you think they have. I had this hand with the author Marshall Miles way back in my early days.

♠AQ109 ♡53 ◇763 ♣AQ108

W	N	E	S
	1♣	Pass	1◇
Pass	1♠	Pass	2NT
Pass	3NT	?	

I looked admiringly at my club and spade honors and thought there was no way this declarer was going to make because I knew declarer wasn't getting any spade or club tricks. I doubled and waited for Marshall's approval.

I got his approval but not very many matchpoints. There was a fly in the ointment. Their side had all of the missing points. My partner, who I was hoping would have stopper in one or both of the red suits, had nothing at all. Marshall led a club like I told him to do but all I got was my two club tricks and my ace of spades. They made an overtrick.

Marshall was sympathetic. "I would have doubled, too," he told me. Thus cheered, we got back to the business of bridge and we won the event. The point of this story? Players who stop in two notrump do not have maximum hands and are often vulnerable to a penalty double as discussed above. Think about it.

STRIPE TAILED APE DOUBLE

This one is perhaps fanciful. You hold this fairly disgusting assortment with the opponents vulnerable.

♠84 ♡Q863 ◇10976 ♣832

Your partner opens with three hearts and the player on your right jumps to four spades. This is a strong jump and from your hand, you are apt to agree that if they wish to bid six or even seven, they will make it. How do you handle this? One thing you can do is pass, hoping that they will misjudge the auction. Another thing you can do is bid five or six or seven hearts, hoping they guess wrong.

The Stripe Tailed Ape is more creative. Double. Stick with me for a few moments before you toss this book in the trash. Let's do a little arithmetic. If they play in four spades making six or seven, they get 680 or 710. This would be a nice result, but really, can this happen? I doubt it. Good opponents (assume they are) will know to go higher. Let's say they bid six spades and make it, perhaps with an overtrick. They score 1430 or 1460. And if they bid seven spades and make it? They get 2210.

Let's go back to that double. If you double and they sit for it, you are minus 1190 if they make six and 1390 if they make an overtrick. If you pass, they rate to bid at least a small slam, and that gets them 1430 points or more. If you double, the worst thing that can happen is 1390. Definitely an improvement.

All very nice. But what if someone redoubles? In that case, the Stripe Tailed Ape reconsiders. He decides that he has enough heart support to raise. In the unlikely event that he gets doubled, he goes down five tricks for 1100, also a considerable improvement over their bidding and making six spades.

The rules for the Stripe Tailed Ape Double are clear.
1. You must think they are cold for slam.
2. You must believe that they will bid it.
3. You must have a safe home, just in case they redouble.
4. Your judgment must be perfect.
5. Your partner needs a sense of humor.

If all these things are in place and if you get away with it, you have a great result, your opponents will be annoyed, and you will have a story that will last a long time.

GAMBLE DOUBLE

I do not know where the name came from. And after learning how it is defined, I remain as confused as ever. However, the concept is interesting. You open with a preempt and the opponents get involved. At some point your RHO cue-bids your suit, and the cue bid is clearly in support of his partner's suit. What should double mean?

Using the double to tell your partner to lead your suit is pretty silly, since your partner is going to lead it anytime he does not have an outstanding choice of his own. Nor do you have to double as a point of honor. Doubling just because you know they cannot make something is one of the silliest doubles around. The next player gains bidding room which can be put to good advantage.

RULE—*Never double unless you have a constructive reason to do so.*

So what should your double mean? Here is a possible auction. You are West with both sides vulnerable.

W	N	E	S
3♡	3♠	Pass	4♡
Dbl			

That four heart cue bid shows a good spade fit, a good hand, and likely includes a heart control, too. If you pass, partner will lead a heart unless he has a better idea. You can help partner form his opinion by doubling four hearts. In this one precise setup, your double says you hope to get a ruff if your partner can guess which suit you want. Since a void is rather unlikely, the double can be used to show a singleton.

♠87 ♡KQJ9764 ◇J109 ♣3

After your opening three heart bid you hear the auction above. LHO bids spades and RHO cue-bids four hearts. By doubling this you greatly improve your chances of setting a slam. Perhaps your partner can lead the ace and another club. Perhaps he can lead a club and get in with the ace of spades. Then he can give you a ruff. This sounds good if it works. But keep in mind that your partner may not guess which suit you want. If he leads diamonds it may cost a trick, and if your opponents are in a slam, it may be a trick you cannot afford to lose.

PENALTY DOUBLES

Winning bridge requires that you compete aggressively. This is the rule that winning players follow. It stands to reason that if your opponents bid aggressively all the time, there will be some ripe moments for you to pick a plum. But you have to know when and how to do it.

The topic of penalty doubles is one of the most difficult that I have ever attempted to translate into print. What makes a penalty double the right bid? There are some obvious situations such as when you have a ton of trumps or they are saving at the five level. But when should you double in ordinary competitive situations? This is a harder question. I would like to give you a half dozen rules which would solve all problems. But I can't. It strikes me that knowing when to make a penalty double depends on judgment as well as rules. Taking the view that this is a correct statement, I am going to present a large number of example hands in the form of a quiz.

Many of the themes come from my *Topics on Bridge, Set Two.* The hands themselves are mostly new ones. I suggest that if you find the topic of penalty doubles interests you, getting your hands on the *Topics on Bridge, Set Two* will give you access to many more examples and specific considerations.

Following is a selection of hands where you might wish to make a penalty double.

W	N	E	S
		1♡	2♢
2♡	3♢	Pass	Pass
?			

♠K1076 ♡1094 ♢Q104 ♣A83

Double. You have way too much to pass, and you do not have a fourth heart. Continuing to the three level with just three trumps is bad. You have to do it occasionally, but having three trumps is a distinct warning signal. On defense you have two certain winners, and your king of spades is likely to be a third. You should expect to set three diamonds two tricks more often than not.

♠82 ♡Q1063 ◊J864 ♣K95

Don't double. You have one of the best reasons to double, four of their trumps, but you have a powerful reason not to double. You have four hearts, your side's trumps. Facing a known singleton diamond and holding four hearts, you are entitled to bid three hearts. While you don't have much, it all rates to be working.

♠82 ♡Q106 ◊J864 ♣K952

This hand is identical to the one above but with one little change. I took away the three of hearts and gave you a small club in return. With this change, you should pass. The difference between three card support and four card support is huge. Point count does not reflect the value of a fourth trump. I estimate it to be the equivalent of a trick in some layouts. If you want to double three diamonds you are welcome to try, but I vote against it. For the record, I would guess that you are more likely to set three diamonds than to make three hearts.

W	N	E	S
		1♡	Pass
2♡	Pass	Pass	3♣
?			

♠AJ2 ♡K62 ◊10863 ♣J74

A tough choice. I would double. Any time someone passes and then balances, they are out on a limb. South is going to be disappointed in the number of points his partner has. You have nine high card points, far more than the five or so you might have on other hands.

155

Compare the differences in these two scenarios.

Case One

W	N	E	S
		1♡	Pass
2♡	Pass	Pass	3♣
?			

Case Two

W	N	E	S
		1♡	Pass
2♡	3♣	Pass	Pass
?			

Which auction shows the better hand? Clearly the second sequence shows a better hand. What this means is that you can take liberties against someone who balances which you wouldn't take against someone who overcalled. South is balancing, which makes his bid suspect.

This double is cooperative. If your partner has weak defense and good shape, he may pull the double. He knows (most of the time) that you have only three trumps for him, which will be a factor in his decision. You should not double if you hate the idea of your partner bidding three hearts. A double by you does ask his opinion. If he believes that defending is a bad idea, he will pull the double. Since he may pull the double, you should not double if you have a totally unsuitable hand. For instance, if you have the KQJ43 of their suit and no other high card and no shape, just passing rates to be best.

W	N	E	S
		1♡	Pass
2♡	Pass	Pass	3◊
?			

♠82 ♡J105 ◊AQ763 ♣J63

Double. Occasionally I see someone pass with a hand like this. They end up setting three diamonds a trick or two and they get a lousy score. Why did they pass? "I didn't want them to run to a better contract."

Not to worry. At least not on this hand. If they can run to a better contract, it will be a small miracle. If, for instance, they are better off in spades, why has this suit not come to light yet? Even if they have a spade contract, it is not likely that they will find it now.

Note that your inactivity may get you a bad score if you set them undoubled, and the penalty turns out to be less than the value of your partscore. When opportunity knocks, you should listen. Here is the kind of hand where you know you can set an opponent but should not double.

W	N	E	S
		1♣	Pass
2♣	Pass	Pass	2◇
?			

♠32 ♡72 ◇QJ864 ♣KJ43

Pass. You can set them badly in two diamonds but doubling is not wise. They rate to have a better home and the bidding is low enough that they may find it. Consider also that your hand may be worth four tricks against diamonds. Against hearts or spades, your diamond values may be worthless. You might not take a single trick against a heart or spade contract.

W	N	E	S
		1♡	2NT
3♡	4♣	Pass	Pass
?			

♠AJ52 ♡10864 ◇J2 ♣K98

The Unusual Notrump convention is one of the more popular conventions in use and it is also one of the most abused conventions in use. Players make lots of bad bids in the name of the Unusual Notrump and you should be able to take advantage of them. Here, I would double four clubs.

It is likely that he has a piece of junk. You have nine high card points, including the ace of spades and the king of clubs (both excellent defensive cards), opposite an opening bid. This suggests the opponents are bidding on a little shape and a lot of nerve. Note that doubling four clubs may not succeed. But note also that if you don't double and they make it, you won't get much for being minus one hundred and thirty points, which is about as bad a result as your side can get. If they go down one or especially two, you will be glad you doubled. This is a matchpoint bid that wins big in the long run.

W	N	E	S
1♠	2NT	3♠	5◇
?			

♠K9764 ♡AKJ ◇85 ♣A62

Double. You have good values with defensive winners. Further, you have a good lead to make. Add in whatever your partner has, and they ought not to make this. This bidding has 'sacrifice' written all over it. South is likely to be overbidding in the hopes of driving you to five spades or perhaps bluffing you into not doubling. This is a fairly standard ploy. If South makes this, you can honestly feel victimized. For the record, when the bidding goes this way, you should always suspect someone of stealing and think about doubling them.

W	N	E	S
1♠	2NT	3♡	5◇
?			

♠KQ9842 ♡6 ◇A5 ♣QJ52

Double. East's three heart bid showed a decent hand, even using the convention called Unusual Vs Unusual. And if you do not use that convention, there is the likelihood that East will bid again if you pass five diamonds. Double will warn East away from bidding again, which suits you fine. It is not that you think you are getting rich off of five diamonds. You are just trying to get a plus score.

W	N	E	S
1◇	2◇	Dbl	2♡
?			

♠A3 ♡J1085 ◇AQ96 ♣K82

Double. This makes the assumption that East's double shows at least ten points, not just some diamonds. As a general principle, I suggest you use East's double in the same way you use redouble when your partner's opening bid is doubled. The double says the hand belongs to your side with the details to be worked out.

If your partner passes the double you will do well. You have the main ingredient of a double, four trumps. Doubles like this can add up quickly when their side can't find a home. If South, for instance, has just two hearts, it won't be fun for him.

What do you lead, by the way, if two hearts doubled is passed out? A trump!

W	N	E	S
		1♣	1♠
Dbl*	2♠	Pass	Pass
?			*Negative

♠J104 ♡AQ73 ◇KJ106 ♣J3

Double, but with the understanding that you are merely saying you have more points than your original Negative Double promised. This is not a penalty double (see the earlier discussion of Negative Doubles). This double normally shows ten or more points and usually includes two or three cards in their suit. This hand is one or two points over a minimum for a repeat double.

W	N	E	S
		1♠	2◇
2♡	3◇	4♡	5◇
?			

♠83 ♡Q8752 ◇KJ ♣KQJ4

Double. Pretty clear. Aside from the possibility of getting a nice number, you do not want to get higher unless your partner insists on it. If you make a forcing pass, you risk playing at the five level. Your diamond honors may prove worthless if East has a singleton diamond, but they will be worth a trick on defense.

If five hearts is your best contract, it is because your partner has a quality hand and when he has that hand, he is allowed to bid five hearts. Your double is an opinion, not a command.

W	N	E	S
		1♡	Pass
1♠	2♣	2◇	Pass
2♠	3♣	Pass	Pass
?			

♠A107643 ♡3 ◇832 ♣A94

Double. This is an excellent matchpoint double and probably worthwhile at IMPs too. You have shown your spades, and you know partner will lead them, unless he has a very clear alternative. You can offer two aces on defense and may get a heart ruff or two. Perhaps your partner can ruff a spade. This double could result in down three for a five hundred point penalty.

W	N	E	S
1♣	Pass	1♠	Pass
2♣	Pass	Pass	2♡
?			

♠7 ♡Q982 ◇A3 ♣AK9854

Double. Do not be afraid to double low level contracts. This is especially true when your opponents are balancing. In today's bidding world, there are some players who refuse to let you play a low level contract. Punish them for this silly view. You have four likely tricks, perhaps five if your partner has anything in hearts. And why should he not? South is bidding a little on speculation, since if he had a real hand he would have bid earlier.

W	N	E	S
		1♣	Pass
1♡	Pass	1NT	Pass
Pass	2♠	Pass	Pass
?			

♠J107 ♡AK863 ◇Q107 ♣83

Double. Between you and your partner, you have around twenty-two high card points. East probably has three spades which means your side has almost as many trumps as they do. One good thing about this hand; if your partner does not know what to lead, he will lead a heart and that will suit you fine. You will know how to continue as soon as you see the dummy.

W	N	E	S
			1♠
Pass	Pass	2♡	2♠
?			

♠A8543 ♡Q7 ◇K73 ♣J109

Pass. As important as it is to know when to double is knowing when not to double. East made a reopening bid, not an overcall. He does not promise much. South knows his partner is weak, but still bid two spades. You have three potential tricks, but on a bad day, you might have just one. Not enough if your partner bid with a light hand. Incidentally, it is in your interest to play with someone who balances aggressively. Doubling with this hand is a good way to discourage your partner from balancing.

Change the hand to the following and double becomes more reasonable.

♠AJ953 ♡Q7 ◇K73 ♣1098

Now you have the key ingredient for a penalty double, genuine trump tricks. Still, even this hand may not be enough.

W	N	E	S
	1♣	Pass	1♡
Pass	1NT	Pass	2♡
Pass	Pass	2♠	3♡
?			

♠Q84 ♡K742 ◇KQ6 ♣Q63

Pass. This pile of junk isn't going anywhere. If you look at the bidding, you will notice that your partner did not bid over one club. This means he does not have much of a hand. His two spade bid gambled that you would provide some points and some spades. His bid already catered to your having this good a hand. Here is the kind of hand your partner might have to bid this way, along with your hand so you can see what the result is likely to be.

♠Q84 ♡K742 ◇KQ6 ♣Q63

♠K9763 ♡J ◇10842 ♣K92

In this layout, the defender on the right showed opening bid strength. In a spade contract, you rate to lose a couple of spades, a heart, at least one diamond and likely two clubs. This adds up to down a few, doubled if you bid on to three spades.

How do you do if you choose to double three hearts? Not very well. Yes, you might set them a trick for down one but many times they will make it and your partner, who was already stressed enough when he bid two spades, will be even more stressed. When your partner makes a balancing bid, do not double the opponents unless it is clear to do so. If, for instance, you had the KJ107 of hearts, that would make double more rewarding.

W	N	E	S
			1♠
Pass	1NT	Pass	2♣
Pass	2♠	Pass	Pass
?			

♠AKJ96 ♡974 ◊7 ♣AJ86

Double. This is a rare auction where a balancing double of a
partscore is for penalty. You have a two notrump bid to use as
takeout, which means that double is available for penalty, a
little known bidding trick. If you think about this, it is logical. If
two notrump shows the unbid suits, why do you need double to
do the same thing? NOTE that if they had bid hearts and clubs
and reached two hearts, a double would be for takeout.

W	N	E	S
			1♡
Pass	1NT	Pass	2♣
Pass	2♡	Pass	Pass
?			

A double here would be for takeout in order to leave room for
your partner to bid two spades if he wished to.

W	N	E	S
			1♡
2◊	2♡	3◊	3♡
?			

♠KQJ ♡J1063 ◊AQ1065 ♣2

Acceptable to double, at least at matchpoints. This auction
occurs frequently. You overcall and everyone raises. Opener
has a tendency to bid to the three level when he should not. It
is OK to whack him on hands like this, because you have four
of his trumps AND you have a good lead in the king of spades.
These hands sometimes go down a few. One further reason
that they are unlikely to make three hearts is that if opener has
a good enough hand to make three (don't forget that he is
going to run into an unexpected bad break in trumps), he

might have bid four. One last thing in favor of doubling is that if your partner has four diamonds and a singleton heart, he might have bid four diamonds instead of three, assuming you are using preemptive raises of overcalls. You will get more good results than bad ones, so if you have a tough constitution, doubling will prove a winner.

W	N	E	S
			1♡
Pass	2♡	Pass	3♡
Pass	4♡	Pass	Pass
?			

♠KQ ♡QJ108 ♢J10974 ♣82

If you wish to double a voluntarily bid game, you should have unexpected trump tricks. It also helps if the opponents stagger into game as opposed to having a confident sequence. You have two heart tricks and probably a spade trick. Not enough to set four hearts but enough to double it. You have nine high card points. The auction tells you that they have about twenty-three high card points, which tells you that your partner has almost as many points as you. He usually will produce a trick or two. A good gamble.

W	N	E	S	
			1♡	
Pass	3♡*	Pass	4♡	*Limit
?				w/4 trumps

♠QJ6 ♡AQ7 ♢A964 ♣Q84

Pass. Unless your opponents are nuts, they will have distribution to make up for all the points you have. This hand has no surprises for declarer. It is possible that you will set four hearts but not so likely that you should double. Here is the kind of thing that happens to greedy doubles like this.

```
              ♠ A753
              ♡ K963
              ◇ Q2
              ♣J103
♠ QJ6                         ♠ 10984
♡ AQ7                         ♡ 2
◇ A964                        ◇ 873
♣Q84                          ♣K7652
              ♠ K2
              ♡ J10854
              ◇ KJ105
              ♣A9
```

South wins the spade lead and leads the jack of hearts. What is West to do? South will know from the double that West has the two heart honors and will get away with just one heart loser. In fact, when West gets in with his ace of hearts he had better lead a club or South will knock out the ace of diamonds and pitch two of dummy's clubs on the diamonds. An overtrick!

W	N	E	S
			Pass
Pass	1♡	Pass	1♠
Pass	2◇	Pass	2NT
Pass	Pass	?	

♠43 ♡AKJ10 ◇J873 ♣654

Double. North opened in third seat and may have opened lighter than normal. South will have his ten or eleven points but they won't be enough, especially with you sitting over North's heart suit. Your double demands a heart lead. After taking the first trick, you will be able to judge how to continue the defense. It would be a genuine surprise if they made two notrump. (See the Lightner Doubles of Partscores for more on this double.)

W	N	E	S
			1♡
Pass	2♠	Pass	2NT
Pass	3♠	Pass	3NT
Pass	4♣	Pass	4NT
Pass	6NT	?	

♠4 ♡763 ◇A8743 ♣A763

Pass. You can beat six notrump if partner leads a club or a diamond. Since a diamond is his most likely lead, that will set them a trick. Why not double? If you double, your partner will think you want a spade lead, dummy's first bid suit, and if he leads one they may have enough tricks to make six notrump. Here is the entire hand as seen by declarer.

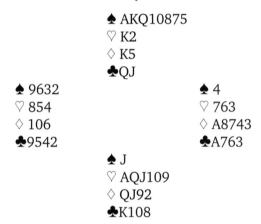

♠ AKQ10875
♡ K2
◇ K5
♣QJ

♠ 9632
♡ 854
◇ 106
♣9542

♠ 4
♡ 763
◇ A8743
♣A763

♠ J
♡ AQJ109
◇ QJ92
♣K108

Wondering what that four club bid was? North thought he was asking for aces and South thought North was showing clubs. The last part of the bidding was a mystery.

Mystery or not, if you double with the East hand, you will get a spade lead and South will make six or seven depending on whether you guess which ace to keep at trick twelve. Better to set six notrump one undoubled trick.

W	N	E	S
1♡	1♠	3♡*	4♠
?			*Limit

♠73 ♡AJ873 ◇AK6 ♣Q95

Double. You opened and got a limit raise from East. You are not in a forcing auction but you do know your side has the large balance of power. I would double four spades on general principle. This hand has three likely defensive tricks, and your partner should offer eight or more high card points to the effort. If you pass, your partner can and likely will pass, and your side will get a modest penalty.

As for making five hearts, that is unlikely. You need partner to have perfect cards for that to be right. In fact, you might not even make four hearts. At this point, doubling and getting three hundred is probably the best you can hope for. At least it is better than getting one hundred. The complete hand looked like this.

```
                    ♠ AQ1082
                    ♡ 109
                    ◇ Q1093
                    ♣J2
  ♠ 73                            ♠ J9
  ♡ AJ873                         ♡ KQ62
  ◇ AK6                           ◇ J852
  ♣Q95                            ♣A104
                    ♠ K654
                    ♡ 54
                    ◇ 74
                    ♣K8763
```

You can set four spades two, which is not as good as making a game, but the good news is that your game will fail as long as the defenders do nothing silly.

Balance of Power Double

Remember the Balance-of-Power Double. When you know you own the majority of the high cards and your opponents are being too frisky, doubling them without any trump tricks may be the answer.

W	N	E	S
1♠	Pass	2♦	3♣
?			

♠AK762 ♡K93 ◇8 ♣Q863

Double them. You have only twelve points, but you have a singleton diamond and four clubs. You have no clear game unless partner is about to support spades, and if he does not intend to do that you probably will do best on defense. You have everything going for you starting with a potential misfit; plus you know your partner has a good hand for his two level response.

W	N	E	S
		1♡	1NT
?			

♠Q983 ♡105 ◇QJ73 ♣KJ3

Double. This is an often overlooked bid. Your partner opens and they overcall one notrump. When you have a nine point hand, your bid should be double unless you have a visible reason not to. Here you have stoppers in all the suits and you are facing an opening bid. Where is declarer going to get any tricks? He has a strong notrump hand facing a dummy with only one or two points. If you reflect on the times when you opened one notrump and played there facing a terrible dummy, you will recall you went down a lot. That is what is going to happen to this declarer in one notrump doubled.

My guideline is to double a one notrump overcall with almost all nine point hands and with many eight point hands. You will come out ahead, I promise, as long as you defend sensibly.

W	N	E	S
			1◇
Dbl	3◇*	3♠	4◇
?			*Preemptive*

♠A84 ♡KQ104 ◇K4 ♣A653

Double. South is not bidding to make, he is just competing. With your good hand and the eight or so points your partner is suggesting, you rate to set four diamonds a couple of tricks. Further, you have only three spades for partner. Your chances for game are not that good. Now, if you had a fourth spade, that would be different.

W	N	E	S
1◇	Dbl	Rdbl	2♣
?			

♠63 ♡A84 ◇KQ98 ♣QJ83

Double. This is the situation the redouble is supposed to create for you. You are not showing a big hand. You are showing four clubs (once in awhile, three is OK) and that you are interested in playing for penalties. Your double is only a strong suggestion. East is not obliged to pass. He is expected to use his judgment and that judgment will be better informed by your double.

W	N	E	S
	1♠	Dbl	4♠
?			

♠64 ♡A5 ◇108653 ♣A964

Double. You have two sure tricks and your partner says he has an opening bid of sorts. North and South are not bidding to make, they are bidding to get in your way. When people try to steal from you, you have to do something other than quietly pass.

W	N	E	S
			1♡
Dbl	Pass	1♠	2♡
?			

♠Q108   ♡AK   ◇A763   ♣AQ52

Double. This is not a penalty double. It is an alertable bid that says you have eighteen or nineteen points with three card support for partner's major. If you had four trumps, you would raise to whatever level your hand was worth. With three you should not raise directly because your partner will misjudge the trumps and might bid again incorrectly.

W	N	E	S
			1♡
Dbl	Pass	1♠	Pass
?			

Change the auction slightly. If opener passes you can show the same hand by making a cue bid of two hearts. It is when opener rebids his suit that you have to resort to the point-showing double. Discuss this bid with your partner. It is very helpful for this type of hand.

W	N	E	S
1NT	2♡	Pass	Pass
Dbl			

W	N	E	S
1NT	Pass	Pass	2♡
Dbl			

No hands. Just a bidding question. You open one notrump and the player on your left bids two hearts. This is passed around to you and you double. Is this for penalty? Next case. You open one notrump and the player on your right reopens with two hearts. You double. Is this for penalty?

My suggestion is that you play double for penalty if you are OVER the bidder and for takeout when you are UNDER the bidder. This means that the first auction is for takeout and the second is for penalty. There are some that think both doubles ought to be for takeout but since that is currently the minority view, I suggest you stick with the way I showed it.

W	N	E	S
1♠	2♡	Pass	4♡
?			

♠Q8763 ♡KQJ ◇A ♣AK108

Pass. The big point of this hand is that a double would be for takeout. If you double, your partner is entitled to bid and that is not what you want. Better to pass and hope for a plus. A double would show something like this hand.

♠AKJ64 ♡— ◇AJ84 ♣KQJ8

Your partner may convert it to penalty by passing, but if he has a long minor or if he has spade support, you would like to hear about it.

W	N	E	S
		1♠	2NT
3NT	4◇	4♠	5◇
?			

♠QJ74 ♡KJ6 ◇Q6 ♣KJ63

First, a short advertisement about the bidding. West's three notrump bid is an extension of Unusual Vs Unusual. Three notrump is not natural, it is an artificial raise saying that you have a BALANCED hand with FOUR or more trumps and game forcing values. This lets partner know what kind of hand you have. With only three card support and game points, you double and then bid game. If you have a shapely hand, you make a splinter bid. When you bid three notrump, you tell partner three important messages at once— your values, your shape, and your trump support.

When South bids five diamonds, you have three options. You can pass to see what East wants to do. You can bid five spades.

You can double. If you pass, it is forcing. You are telling your partner that you are not sure what is right. You need a hand that is clearly willing to go to five spades.

If you bid five spades, you are saying that you know five spades is the right contract. It is rather rare that you can be so sure of this that you make this bid. If you double, you are saying that in light of your first bid, you are not very proud of your hand.

Double is my choice on this hand. You have the points you needed to bid three notrump, but they are not good points. With no aces and some of your values wasted, such as the queen of diamonds, this is a relatively poor hand. Double warns East that you are not happy going to the five level. East is not barred from bidding on, he is just advised that he is to proceed with caution.

WHEN TO PULL A PENALTY DOUBLE

This is a topic that I have never seen in print. Books occasionally talk about penalty doubles, although not nearly enough. But talk about when to pull a penalty double, never. I wish I could come up with some firm guidelines. Sadly, there are hundreds of situations where someone doubles and someone else must decide if they like it. I will give you a few hands and see what principles we can come up with.

W	N	E	S
		1♢	Pass
1NT	2♡	Dbl	Pass
?			

Here are three hands using this auction.

♠K76 ♡104 ♢Q73 ♣Q10986

Pass. The first thing you must think about is whether your partner knows what you have. You said you had six to nine high card points, which you do. You said you had, probably, a balanced hand, which you do. This double is for penalty and you have what you said you had.

♠KJ ♡4 ◇732 ♣QJ98653

Here you have the points you promised, but you do not have a balanced hand and you do have an extreme untold message. It is reasonable to bid three clubs with this hand. Note that you have three diamonds and one heart. Your mild diamond fit is one more hint that you should not sit for this double.

♠K6 ♡Q6 ◇J876 ♣K8642

You might consider going back to diamonds, but since you have a maximum hand with a heart honor and defensive values on the side, sitting for this double is pretty clear cut. One additional point to think about is that on this bidding your partner could have four-four-three-two shape. You would not want to play in a four-three diamond fit.

W	N	E	S
			1♡
2NT	Pass	3◇	3♡
Pass	Pass	Dbl	Pass
?			

♠J10 ♡10 ◇AJ873 ♣K10765

Your partner heard you use the Unusual Notrump, and he said double. What do you have that your partner does not know about?

Well, he knows you have five-five in the minors and that you did not rebid over South's three hearts. You rate to have a minimum hand, which is what you have. Bidding with this is horrible. Even though you have a shapely hand, your partner knows it. His double was made with that information in mind. You don't have a lot of defense but you have everything you promised.

W	N	E	S
			1♡
2NT	3♡	Dbl	Pass
?			

♠2 ♡— ◇QJ10974 ♣KQJ985

Bid three notrump, insisting on partner showing his best minor. You have much more playing strength than normal and much less defense than you might have. It is possible that three hearts doubled is the best spot for you, but running is still wise. You need partner to have one useful high card to make four of a minor, and you have a terrible hand on defense.

♠K ♡4 ◇Q10876 ♣KJ6542

Pass. You have poor quality suits, and you have some defense. Your king of spades, while not looking very nice, may be a big asset on defense. Give your partner the QJ87 of spades and your side has a source of winners. Another way of looking at this is that since your partner did not bid a minor, your best chance of getting a plus score is sitting for the double. By the way, I am not sure that bidding two notrump with this was a good idea. Lousy suits and poor points do not add up to a bid.

W	N	E	S
4♣	4♡	Dbl	Pass
?			

♠4 ♡4 ◇J107 ♣KJ1087643

The whole point of preempting is to hassle the opponents and force them into indiscretions. Your partner's double said they are wrong. How can West be so wise as to know that East made a mistake? A preemptor should preempt and then accept what happens. Even if South redoubled, West should pass. East is still better informed about what West has than West is about what East has. For all West knows, East is about to lead the ace and king and a third spade for West to ruff.

W	N	E	S
1♠	2◇	Pass	Pass
2♠	3◇	Dbl	Pass
?			

♠KQJ9874 ♡43 ◇— ♣KQ109

Bid three spades. You will have a play for this opposite very little and your defense against diamonds is pathetic.

♠AQ108653 ♡A8 ◇3 ♣KJ2

Pass. The huge difference between this hand and the previous one is that you have less playing strength and very good defense. Your hand will not be a disappointment in any way to your partner. Always consider your playing strength AND your defensive strength. If your defensive values are OK, it is usually right to pass. A long suit is not a sufficient reason to run out.

W	N	E	S
		1♡	Dbl
3♡	4♣	Dbl	Pass
?			

♠9764 ♡Q8763 ◇J73 ♣10

Pass. You promised a weak hand and your partner won't expect more. This is another example of a preemptive hand making its bid and then being quiet. One thing you can count on. Your partner is not planning on many heart winners on defense.

W	N	E	S
		1♡	1♠
2♠	3♠	Dbl	Pass
?			

♠92 ♡AQ106 ◇QJ4 ♣QJ87

First, let me explain the bidding. West's cue bid of two spades says he has a game forcing hand with four hearts and a balanced hand. If West had a singleton spade and the same values otherwise, he would have bid three spades to show a singleton. West expects there is a game on for East-West and has to decide whether to sit for the double or to put East into four hearts.

Frankly, it is a bit surprising to hear East double, but he did. East clearly said he prefers to defend three spades doubled rather than play in four hearts. Do you have any reason to overrule this? I would guess not. For one of the few times in this section, I will show you partner's hand.

♠ 92	♠ KQJ
♡ AQ106	♡ KJ953
◇ QJ4	◇ 85
♣QJ87	♣K64

East's judgment on this hand was excellent. He knew his spade values were largely wasted and the rest of his hand was boring. Four hearts does not make and setting three spades is the best result available to East-West.

Certainly, East's double is not a demand, only an opinion. If West had more prime cards, bidding four hearts would be OK.

W	N	E	S
			1♣
Dbl	1♡	1♠	2♡
Pass	Pass	Dbl	Pass
?			

♠KQ93 ♡QJ6 ◇KQ102 ♣73

Bid two spades. Your partner made a free bid of one spade, which is not a strong bid. The best hand he can have is about eight points, perhaps nine. When he doubled two hearts, he was not making a ferocious penalty double so much as a suggestion that he has a maximum one spade bid and probably a couple of hearts.

Your hand is minimum and very weighted in favor of spades. With far less defense against hearts than you might have and with as weak a hand as you can have and with as much in spades as you have, it is clear to run back to two spades. If you had one less spade and one more heart, sitting for the double would be acceptable.

W	N	E	S
1♠	1NT	Dbl	Pass
?			

♠Q6542 ♡AK ◇QJ874 ♣9

Bid two diamonds. The first thing to realize is that East made a penalty double. Some players get it into their heads that this is some kind of Negative Double. Nonsense. This is a penalty double and your first thought should be to pass it. The reasons for bidding here are that you have a minimum, which of itself is not enough reason to run. You also have excellent shape and fear getting a spade lead. You do not want that. You would love a diamond lead or even a heart lead in some layouts. My guess is that you will sit for this double about ninety percent of the time. This hand is one of that ten percent of hands that has a reason to bid.

W	N	E	S
1◇	1♡	1♠	Pass
2♣	2♡	Dbl	Pass
?			

♠K ♡53 ◇AJ1065 ♣A10863

Pass, and happily. One of the keys to such decisions is the quality of your defensive strength. You have aces and you have the king of spades, a likely contributor. Better yet, you have a doubleton heart. This is a plus since it is one less trump for them to have. You may be able to get a spade ruff in addition to the high card tricks your side has. Basically, the big motivation for passing is that you have guaranteed winners on defense.

W	N	E	S
		1♡	1♠
4♡	4♠	Dbl	Pass
?			

♠— ♡J107653 ◇32 ♣QJ1096

You would be forgiven if you pulled this double to five hearts.
With exceptional trumps, a void, and no high card tricks to
offer, you are entitled to run. If you had one spade in your
hand, sitting would be better. You did not promise your partner
anything when you bid four hearts, but you did not imply this
extreme a hand either. In general, if you show your hand and
your partner doubles, you should leave it in. This hand is an
exception.

W	N	E	S
Pass	1♡	1♠	Pass
2◇	2♡	Dbl	Pass
?			

♠5 ♡82 ◇A107653 ♣KJ54

Pass. Two diamonds was not forcing. Your hand is about what
you are expected to have. You have an ace and you have
potential tricks in clubs. Since you have what you promised,
you should pass. Note that you have one spade, a very nice
holding. With a diamond lead to your ace, you will be in a
position to do whatever looks best including returning a spade
in search of ruffs. Anytime you have an ace in a suit your
partner is expected to lead, you know you can win the trick and
choose what to do next. If you have a lesser suit, declarer may
win an early trick, and then he gets to decide what to do next.

REDOUBLES

The redouble is one of the last frontiers of bidding. Given that I see a new convention almost every time I play, I would expect to see more conventions with 'Redouble' in their name. Perhaps it is because an error with the redouble can lead to such spectacular scores that it has been treated so gingerly. The number of meanings for redouble is extensive. I'll cover just a few.

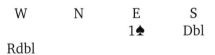

W	N	E	S
		1♠	Dbl
Rdbl			

The auction that comes up the most starts with a one bid, a takeout double, and a redouble. Less frequent auctions are those that start with a preempt. West's redouble is pretty standard stuff. Ninety percent of the world uses the redouble to show ten or more points. I have a few thoughts on this to help clear up some possible accidents. If you redouble, you normally have one of four things in mind.

1. You hope to double the opponents.
2. You have support for partner without enough trumps to make an artificial raise immediately.
3. You expect to bid notrump along the way if you can't double the opponents.
4. Rarely, you will redouble and then bid a suit later. This is forcing.

If you have a good hand with a higher ranking suit than the one your partner opened, it is almost always best to bid your suit (forcing) and then continue the auction in normal fashion. Redoubling with all good hands can cause problems later.

Here are a few example hands with my suggestions.

W	N	E	S
		1♡	Dbl
?			

♠108   ♡J106   ◇AQ874   ♣K82

Redouble. You expect to raise hearts next. By redoubling before raising hearts, you deny four of them. With four or more hearts you show support immediately, often using something called the Jordan Two Notrump bid. This Jordan bid is occasionally called the Irregular Redouble. See the example below.

♠J1075   ♡QJ84   ◇AQ8   ♣87

Bid two notrump. After a MAJOR suit opening bid and a takeout double, a jump to two notrump promises four or more trumps and limit raise or better values.

♠J54   ♡32   ◇AJ84   ♣KJ94

Redouble. You hope that you can double them. Failing that, you probably will bid notrump somewhere along the way.

♠AQJ73   ♡73   ◇93   ♣K1097

One spade. It is almost always best to bid a higher ranking suit than opener's when you have values to redouble. One spade is forcing, and if you subsequently bid clubs, that is forcing too. Redoubling here may force you to show your spades at the three level or higher.

W	N	E	S
		2♡	Dbl
Rdbl			

Whether East opens with a two level or higher preempt, a redouble says that you think your partner will make the contract. It also implies that you would like to double the opponents when they bid. When this auction occurs, your partner is allowed to get into the doubling, too.

WEST	EAST
♠ AQ763	♠ 9
♡ 9	♡ KJ10753
◇ J104	◇ A85
♣AK84	♣1073

West is pretty sure that two hearts doubled will make, and his redouble just adds to the urgency placed on the opponents. When North runs to three diamonds, East doubles it. East is not likely to have four diamonds so doubling with three is fine. What East has is a maximum weak two bid with as much defense as he normally would have. Note that West is not certain that he can double diamonds himself, so he is happy to hear East do that for him.

If you redouble after partner's one bid, you need agreements about followup bids. For instance, if you redouble and bid a new suit, is it forcing or invitational? If you redouble and the opponents bid at the one level, does your side have to keep bidding? Is there any level that they can bid to where your side can retire from the bidding? For instance:

♠64 ♡KQ7 ◇K10542 ♣QJ3

W	N	E	S
		1♡	Dbl
Rdbl	3♠	Pass	Pass
?			

You had intended to follow your redouble with a heart raise. Do you have to bid again now that they have bid three spades?

I can tell you that if you read any book on bridge, you won't find this topic mentioned. The authors either do not address the question, or they purposely ignore it because they do not want to deal with it. Take your partnership, for example. Have you ever discussed these questions? If not, you have company.

One reason that it is not discussed is that it is difficult to know what to do when the opponents compete. I offer this simple guideline that you are welcome to change. Play that when you redouble, your side is obliged to bid if they bid lower than three of opener's suit, unless you choose to double them first.

W	N	E	S
		1◇	Dbl
Rdbl			

After this start, if the opponents bid up to three clubs, your side must bid again or double them. If they bid to three hearts or higher, your side is allowed to get out of the auction. This is not a difficult rule to follow as long as your initial bid is sensible. This hand appeared earlier.

♠AQJ73 ♡73 ◇93 ♣K1097

I stated that if your partner opens one heart and the next player doubles, it is better to bid one spade. If you redouble, you may hear them bid to three diamonds. That will force you to bid three spades, which will be forcing. You do not want to force at the three level. By bidding one spade with this hand, you keep later problems to a minimum. You will still have problems but fewer of them.

WE-CAN-MAKE-IT REDOUBLE AND THE SOS REDOUBLE

Some redoubles mean exactly what they sound like. An opponent doubles and you redouble to say you expect to make the contact. You have to be sure that if you redouble, your partner knows your intentions and does not think you are making an SOS Redouble. Because these two redoubles go hand in hand, I will touch on both at the same time.

Let's assume you have been doubled for penalty. A We-Can-Make-It Redouble says that the redoubler is sure the contract is making; he is raising the stakes considerably by redoubling. The SOS Redouble says that the redoubler wants to find a better home and asks partner to start looking elsewhere.

Here is an assortment of redoubles with my thoughts. Assume no one is vulnerable and that North's or South's double is for penalty.

W	N	E	S
		1NT	Dbl
Rdbl			

Right away we run into uncertainty. This redouble, classically, shows eight or more points and says that one notrump, doubled and redoubled, is a fine contract. If you play redouble this way, you are doing what half of the world does. But, there are other meanings that can be assigned to a redouble. A popular scheme of escaping from one notrump doubled is to play that redouble asks partner to bid two clubs, over which responder will show his suit.

♠32 ♡QJ753 ◇765 ♣873

Using this trick, you would redouble and then bid two hearts over partner's two club bid. In conjunction with this redouble trick, a bid of a new suit by you over the double says you have that suit and a higher one. You are trying to escape from one notrump doubled.

♠107653 ♡J4 ◇6 ♣J10763

With this hand you would bid two clubs, showing clubs and a higher ranking suit. I leave the details of this escape mechanism to the reader. Suffice it to say that if you play DONT over their notrumps, this should be very familiar.

W	N	E	S
		1NT	Pass
Pass	Dbl	Pass	Pass
Rdbl			

A sensible rule is that when you are in the passout seat of a doubled contract, you should play a redouble as SOS. If you think you can make your contract, just pass and take whatever you can get from making it. There will be some auctions where this rule is not valid, but those auctions will include enough bidding that your intentions are clear.

W	N	E	S
		1♡	Pass
Pass	Dbl	Pass	Pass
Rdbl			

Since you could pass one heart doubled, your redouble is defined as SOS.

♠10986 ♡— ◇10876 ♣Q10874

Redouble to tell East that you do not want to play in one heart doubled. He will bid another suit if he is on your wavelength.

W	N	E	S
		1♠	Pass
Pass	Dbl	Pass	Pass
?			

♠8 ♡QJ763 ◇1098742 ♣3

Redouble. If East bids clubs and is doubled again, you will redouble again, showing the red suits. If your partner bids one notrump, you can continue to redouble until your partner bids a red suit or you could bid two diamonds, which would imply diamonds and hearts.

W	N	E	S
	1♡	2♣	Pass
Pass	Dbl	Pass	Pass
?			

♠K10653 ♡3 ◇1076432 ♣2

Redouble. In this case you are showing two suits and praying that you have a better contract than two clubs, doubled.

W	N	E	S
		1♡	Pass
2♡	Dbl	Pass	Pass
Rdbl			

This is an unexpected sequence. West's redouble says he has full confidence in his raise, and North-South have made an error in judgment. You do not often bid to a contract on your own and then redouble to say you think there is a better place.

W	N	E	S
			1♡
2◇	Pass	Pass	Dbl
Rdbl			

West has not been passed out in a doubled contract yet. It may happen if North decides to pass, but for now, he does not know if the bidding is going to stop. His redouble therefore shows a maximum hand with a good suit and says he is not ready to give up on the hand yet.

♠AK ♡2 ◇AQ8765 ♣A864

I held this hand in an important team match. The bidding went as shown and I redoubled to show a super overcall and to invite my partner into the bidding if he felt he had any useful values. This went down one thousand points when my LHO turned up with the KJ1092 of diamonds, and my partner had a totally useless hand. At least my partner knew what my redouble meant.

W	N	E	S
		1NT	Pass
3NT	Dbl	Pass	Pass
Rdbl			

This redouble says that North made an error. An aside here. If North is using one of those Lightner Doubles that I discussed earlier, that fact should have been alerted.

W	N	E	S
		4♡	Dbl
Rdbl			

West is showing a hand that expects to make four hearts. He also has a good defensive hand that intends to double the opponents if they decide to bid something.

♠AK93 ♡Q ◇AJ7 ♣QJ1096

Opposite a four heart opening bid, there should be ten or more tricks available. The redouble will get you a huge score if it is passed out, and if they bid, you are ready with the hammer.

REDOUBLE AFTER A NEGATIVE DOUBLE

W	N	E	S
	1♡	1♠	Dbl*
Rdbl			*Negative

A redouble after a Negative Double is not SOS. It says you have a good hand of some sort but without any genuine support. If you had real spade support, you would cue-bid two hearts. In the treatment I like best a redouble says I have at least ten points and exactly two of my partner's suit. This treatment can be used when your partner makes a two level overcall, also.

THEY DOUBLE A CUE BID, YOU'RE ON THE WAY TO SLAM

♠AQJ87 ♡2 ◇AQ6 ♣AJ54

W	N	E	S
1♠	Pass	3♠	Pass
4♣	Dbl	Pass	Pass
?			

Partner made a limit raise, which got you to thinking of a slam. When four clubs got doubled, slam looked dimmer. With partner denying the ace of hearts it looks like four spades might be the limit. I would bid four spades and expect to be high enough. Let's try this auction again with a different bid from partner.

W	N	E	S
1♠	Pass	3♠	Pass
4♣	Dbl	Rdbl	Pass
?			

Do you have an agreement about East's redouble? You should. It is not a common moment in your life but when it occurs, it is an important one. East is saying that he has second round control of clubs, which is good news for you. Knowing that you do not have a gaping hole in clubs, you can afford to cue-bid four diamonds. Here is the rest of the bidding.

W	N	E	S
1♠	Pass	3♠	Pass
4♣	Dbl	Rdbl	Pass
4◇	Pass	5◇	Pass
6♠	Pass	Pass	Pass

♠ AQJ87	♠ K1042
♡ 2	♡ Q8643
◇ AQ6	◇ KJ8
♣AJ54	♣2

187

Six spades is an excellent spot. With some defenses, it is cold. Even with a trump lead you are a favorite to bring it home. The point of this hand is not the play, however, but the bidding. In the second auction when responder redoubled, opener learned something useful. Further, it left room for opener to make another cue bid of four diamonds. After that, responder cue-bid the king of diamonds and opener just bid the slam, knowing that the ace of hearts was missing.

Was this bidding reasonable? I would say yes. Some players view a double as a scary event but it need not be so. If you have a redouble available to add to your cue-bidding structure, you can bid hands like this to the best contract. Note that if North had not doubled four clubs, the bidding would have been harder for you. Remember this the next time you feel like making a frivolous double of a cue bid. On this hand, North was going to be on lead so his double was even more wasteful than normal. Was he reminding himself to lead a club?

THEY DOUBLE A JACOBY TRANSFER

W	N	E	S
1NT	Pass	2♡	Dbl
Rdbl			

There are two treatments that I know exist. In the first, the redouble says you want to play in this contract.

♠108 ♡AQ107 ◇AK7 ♣K1074

You might redouble with this hand to offer two hearts as a place to play. If your partner has two or three hearts and seven high card points, you should be able to make eight tricks with hearts as trump for a sensational score. If your partner does not like hearts, his choices tend to be two spades on weak hands, two notrump with invitational hands, and three notrump with good hands. All well and good.

In practice, not much ever happens with this treatment except for the rare moment when you play two hearts redoubled, making. Oh, yes. You may have an occasional hand where two hearts, redoubled, goes down. It can happen. Since the redouble for penalty seldom gains, I lean towards the second treatment. In this method, a redouble says that you have a good hand for partner's major but not so good that you can jump to the three level.

W	N	E	S
1NT	Pass	2♡	Dbl
Rdbl			

♠QJ8 ♡A7 ♢AQ1084 ♣K93

This is a good hand for spades, but not so good that you want to get higher than two spades facing a minimum response. Here is a list of possible bids for opener after the transfer bid is doubled.

Rdbl   A good hand with three trumps or a hand with four trumps that is good, but not good enough to jump. If RHO doubles a two heart transfer bid, you might redouble with both of these hands.

♠J83 ♡AQ43 ♢K7 ♣AQ108
♠Q1075 ♡K85 ♢AJ5 ♣KQJ

The first hand has sixteen nice points with three trumps and the second has an ordinary sixteen points with bad shape but with four trumps. Both of these hands are worth a redouble. This way, your partner will know you like your hand somewhat and can use that information in the bidding.

Pass   Only two spades. It does not matter whether you have a maximum or a minimum.

♠Q7 ♡QJ86 ♢KQJ8 ♣A64
♠K6 ♡J95 ♢KQJ7 ♣AK97

If partner knows you have just two spades, he will be able to judge the auction better than when he does not know.

2♠   Three or four spades but a minimum hand.

♠J73 ♡KJ6 ◇QJ1096 ♣AK
♠AQ73 ♡Q76 ◇Q94 ♣KQ2

Again, your partner learns something important. He learns you have genuine support but also a relatively bad hand. This may keep him from making a close game try, thus keeping you in a safe partscore.

3♠   A maximum hand with four trumps, quality points, and some shape.

♠AJ85 ♡K5 ◇AQ5 ♣K742

This is a nice three spade bid. Your partner can go on to game with seven point hands that would not have bid over a two spade bid.

♠QJ87 ♡QJ9 ◇KQJ ♣KQ2

This is a redouble, not a three spade bid. You have good spades but your points are not good ones, and you have poor shape. Three spades would be an error.

This structure comes up frequently, and I promise it will be useful in your game bidding. There will be many occasions where you stop safely at the two level, and a few where you bid nice games that might be hard to reach otherwise.

W	N	E	S
1NT	Pass	2◇	Dbl
Pass	Pass	?	

East tried to transfer to hearts. South doubled, and West refused the transfer. There is a nice bidding trick that East can use which opens some extra avenues for East-West.

Pass   A remarkable choice. East may do this if he has four diamonds and some points. Opener's pass says he has only two hearts but it says nothing about diamonds.

♠83 ♡K7653 ◊J865 ♣K2

East can try for a top by passing two diamonds, doubled. It will make often enough that it is worth a try.

2♡   East can bid two hearts, ending the auction. He might wish to play in hearts from his side of the table with something in diamonds if he does not want the lead going through his hand.

♠874 ♡Q9732 ◊Q73 ♣98

Two hearts from your side may be better than two hearts from your partner's side.

Rdbl   East can redouble, which tells opener to bid two hearts. This is how East gets opener to play the hand.

3♣   This is a special bid that can occur only after the transfer is doubled and opener refuses to accept it. A new suit at the three level shows a weak five-five hand and is not forcing. Responder knows opener does not have three cards in the transfer suit, so he rates to have a fit for responder's second suit.

♠4 ♡J8653 ◊J3 ♣Q10974

East can bid three clubs and will play it there. A sensible choice.

If responder wants to transfer to the major and then bid a new suit and have it be forcing, he transfers and then redoubles to force opener to take the transfer. Then responder bids his second suit and the bidding continues along normal forcing lines.

♠KJ1076 ♡3 ◊763 ♣AQ105

With no intervention, East would transfer to spades and then bid clubs, looking for the best game contract. If the transfer bid is doubled and opener does not accept, this auction occurs.

W	N	E	S
1NT	Pass	2♡	Dbl
Pass	Pass	Rdbl	Pass
2♠	Pass	3♣	

East's sequence, redoubling and then bidding a new suit, is game forcing.

INFORMATORY REDOUBLE

Here is a treatment that I first showed in my book, *The Complete Book on Overcalls*. Players who have read that book know about this trick, but it has not spread very far. I know because whenever it comes up at the table, someone notes that this must be a new idea.

W	N	E	S
			1♠
2♣	Pass	2♠	Dbl
Rdbl			

West's redouble is the key. On the auction here, East has an assortment of possible intentions. Usually he has club support but he may have other things in mind. It is possible that he wants to see if three notrump is a viable contract. Sorting out a stopper in their suit, spades in this case, has a high priority. This is what the redouble is all about. West is saying he has a good overcall and additionally says he has one of the following.

1.   I have a full stopper in spades, opener's suit.
2.   I have a partial stopper in spades, opener's suit.

If responder is interested in notrump, he knows he can bid notrump if he has half a stopper or better. If he has nothing in opener's suit, he finds some other bid. On the next round, opener can bid notrump with a full stopper, so notrump won't get lost when responder can't bid it himself. Here are three hands using this treatment.

W	N	E	S
			1♠
2♣	Pass	2♠	Dbl
Rdbl	Pass	3♣	Pass
Pass	Pass		

♠ J63		♠ 752
♡ A3		♡ KJ84
◇ 83		◇ AQ9
♣AK10986		♣J42

West shows he has something in spades but East is not interested. He bids three clubs, thus implying that he has a normal cue-bid response.

W	N	E	S
			1♠
2♣	Pass	2♠	Dbl
Rdbl	Pass	3NT	Pass
Pass	Pass		

♠ Q5		♠ 10874
♡ 42		♡ AJ
◇ AK3		◇ Q874
♣KJ9875		♣AQ6

When West shows a sound overcall with something in spades, East just shoots it out in three notrump. Without this agreement, you would probably miss three notrump unless someone made a lucky guess.

	W	N	E	S
				1♠
	2♣	Pass	2♠	Dbl
	Rdbl	Pass	3♣	Pass
	3NT	Pass	Pass	Pass

♠ K63	♠ 75
♡ J6	♡ Q953
◇ A3	◇ KJ84
♣KQJ975	♣A102

West tried to get East to play the hand in case he had something like the Q2 of spades but when East denied interest in notrump, West just bid it.

You will find other auctions are possible after this informatory redouble. This is a useful tool that can grow as you become comfortable with it.

DOUBT-SHOWING REDOUBLE

Are you going for 800 or 1100 now and then? Try using the Doubt-Showing Redouble and you will start enjoying results like minus 1600 or 2200 instead.

♠ AKJ	♠ Q1063
♡ 74	♡ J653
◇ K87	◇ AJ3
♣AQJ92	♣103

W	N	E	S
1♣	Pass	1♡	Pass
2NT	Pass	3NT	Dbl
Pass	Pass	Pass	

Here is the problem. West reaches three notrump on a normal sequence and South doubles to ask for a heart lead. When it is all over, West has lost the first five heart tricks and later loses a club trick for minus five hundred. Pretty gross stuff. Was this the only result possible? I can tell you that it is a result that would be fairly frequent in a field that knows about lead directing doubles.

With some fear I offer the Doubt-Showing Redouble. It works like this. When an opponent doubles your three notrump bid for the lead of a specific suit, a redouble says you are worried about that suit. On this hand West would redouble with his two little hearts and East would then pass only with a stopper and run without one. This nasty little convention can lead to some pretty horrendous results.

Say, for instance, that South has doubled with just four hearts. Now it is possible that you can make three notrump with a heart lead. If so, you will have traded in a huge plus score for a much less useful score. It also means that you will lose some juicy redoubles when you know you can make your bid but can't redouble for fear that your partner will take it out.

Here is one more sample of this creation at work. You will notice that it took one strange piece of science to give you this problem. (Don't try this at home!)

♠ K3		♠ AJ104	
♡ 53		♡ Q98	
◇ AQ109753		◇ K82	
♣K3		♣AQ9	

W	N	E	S
1◇	Pass	1♠	2♡
2NT	Pass	3NT	Dbl
Rdbl	Pass	5◇	Pass
Pass	Pass		

The auction will be completely unfamiliar to anyone except nouveau scientists. The first round of the bidding is normal but after South's two heart bid, it gets interesting.

West's two notrump is the good-bad toy, something I discussed briefly in the section on Negative Doubles. West wants to bid three diamonds but not get East excited. You can do this by having the agreement that a direct three diamond bid shows a bigger hand, so with the actual hand you bid two notrump, nominally forcing three clubs from your partner. Now when you follow with three diamonds, partner knows that you have only a competitive three diamond bid.

However, East has such a huge hand that he does not want to miss game, so he bids three notrump (hoping that West has something in hearts). West's redouble is the Doubt-Showing variety saying he is really worried about hearts for notrump. With hearts stopped, East should feel free to pass, but he must not leave three notrump in without a sure stopper. East does not have one, so the partnership gets to the game that they should have been in from the start.

The Doubt-Showing Redouble shows two or three little cards in the danger suit. With a doubleton ten or better, it is probably better to pass. Partner should know enough to use good judgment now. Fun stuff.

There is a case of this convention being used in World Championship play where the opening lead missed the mark by eleven tricks. The problem was that the opening leader did not know which suit the double called for, and he guessed wrong. It was a matter of both sides having eleven tricks. Which side took their eleven was a function of how well the opening leader did.

A final thought regarding Doubt-Showing Redoubles of three notrump. It is rare to have an interest in redoubling three notrump. It is not a daily event. When it does happen, though, the partnership must know when it is Doubt-Showing and when it is for real. For example:

♠J4 ♡A8 ◇AKQJ106 ♣A83

W	N	E	S
1◇	1♠	1NT	Pass
3NT	Dbl	Pass	Pass
?			

Redouble. This is not a Doubt-Showing Redouble because your side learned of North's spade suit and still bid notrump. East's one notrump bid promised a spade stopper. No doubt here. What North is doing is unknown, but you know that he is wrong. Redouble and get out your pen. Figuring out what the result is worth may take awhile.

For the record, these are the combined hands.

```
                    ♠ AK985
                    ♡ 972
                    ◇ 3
                    ♣KQJ10

    ♠ J4                        ♠ Q1062
    ♡ A8                        ♡ KQJ
    ◇ AKQJ106                   ◇ 74
    ♣A83                        ♣9764

                    ♠ 73
                    ♡ 106543
                    ◇ 9852
                    ♣52
```

North had planned to take the first spade and switch to clubs. He saw five potential tricks and made a daring double. West's hand was a disappointment to North, and three notrump came home with a satisfying overtrick.

If West fears to redouble because East may think that it is the Doubt-Showing Redouble, then he may pass. Of course, three notrump doubled with an overtrick is a nice score, but making an overtrick in three notrump, redoubled, is even nicer and it will carry some weight the next time you play these opponents.

Mike Lawrence has written an extensive list of books covering many topics that you will not find discussed elsewhere. Many are classics.

Complete Book on Balancing	$11.95
Complete Book on Hand Evaluation	$11.95
Complete Book on Overcalls	$11.95
Complete Book on Takeout Doubles	$12.95
Contested Auctions	$14.95
D.O.N.T	$6.00
Dynamic Defense	$11.95
Falsecards	$17.00
Handbook of Partnership Understandings	$5.95
How to Play Card Combinations	$12.95
How to Read Your Opponents' Cards	$12.95
I Fought the Law (of Total Tricks)	$17.95
Judgement at Bridge	$11.95
Opening Leads	$19.95
Passed Hand Bidding	$13.95
Play a Swiss Team of Four with Mike Lawrence	$9.95
Play Bridge with Mike Lawrence	$11.95
The Two Over One System	$12.95
The Uncontested Auction	$13.95
Topics on Bridge II	$40.00

Mike has also created a number of software programs that will teach you how to play bridge. Instead of watching your computer play, perhaps making bad bids or plays, and never getting any insight or instruction, Mike's software lets you play and defend hands with him sitting at your shoulder. He gives you helpful hints and helps you solve the problems as they arise.

Conventions	Windows	$40.00
Counting at Bridge	Windows	$34.95
Counting at Bridge II	Windows	$34.95
Defense	Windows	$34.95
Mike Lawrence's Bridge Dealer	Windows	$50.00
Private Bridge Lessons I	Windows	$34.95
Private Bridge Lessons II	Windows	$34.95
Two Over One	Windows	$34.95

Information on these can be found on Mike's website,

www.michaelslawrence.com

Or if you wish, please contact Mike by email,

77bridge@best.com,

or by phone, (615) 221-9952.

Would you like personal classes with Mike? Lectures or supervised classes are available.

Would you like to be able to send Mike an email with your question? Mike also does email consultation.

For information on these services just contact Mike by phone or email.